THE ART OF THE KILL

By Pete Bonanni

Spectrum HoloByte
Alameda, California

Author: Pete Bonanni

Editors: Howard Bornstein, Robert Giedt and Marisa Ong

Graphic Designer: Carrie Galbraith

Illustrator: Lawrence Kevin

Product Management: Steve Blankenship

Product Marketing: Neil Johnston and Kathryn Lynch

Special Thanks: Anthony Chiang, Joseph Colligan, Jack Gibbons, Patrick Gost, Lucija Kordić, Gilman Louie, Joy Matsuura, Planned Marketing Solutions, Russel Reiss and Gary Stottlemyer

Spectrum HoloByte
2490 Mariner Square Loop
Alameda, CA 94501

Printed in the United States of America
10 9 8 7 6 5 4 3 2 1

Table of Contents

Foreword

Art of the Kill has been designed to teach you the fundamentals of Basic Fighter Maneuvers (BFM). As the name implies, BFM is the cornerstone of tactical fighter aviation. Since its principles are rooted in the laws of physics, geometry and aerodynamics, they are non-negotiable and cannot be finessed.

Depending upon what your expectations were when you purchased *Art of the Kill*, a couple of learning outcomes are possible. If you watch the videotape only once as you flip through this book, you will probably be mildly entertained and may even retain a few basic principles of BFM. If on the other hand, you read this book in conjunction with repeated reviews of Pete Bonanni's excellent videotaped presentations, you'll learn and understand the imperatives of how to maneuver aircraft in a visual engagement environment. I can guarantee you that such knowledge will serve you well.

There is a growing myth that the technological sophistication of the modern fighter aircraft has turned aerial combat into a "push button" form of high-tech warfare. So you may be wondering why, in an era of pulse-doppler radar, low observable technology and sophisticated missiles, should one devote time and energy to learning something as old-fashioned as BFM. Why not simply "shoot 'em in the face" before they ever see you? More than a few sincere advocates have been making that argument for years. As an aspiring fighter pilot in the 1950s, I first heard the same *siren song* when the F-86 was armed with the original AIM-9 Sidewinder missile. The story line then was that missiles of that ilk, used in combination with radar control, were going to make "dogfighting" a thing of the past with the fighter pilot being relegated to a role of pushing "magic buttons" upon command. It didn't happen then; it didn't happen with the introduction of the "Century Series" supersonic fighters; it didn't happen with the development of F-15s, F-16s, F/A-18s or any of the other first-line fighters of today; and if I were a betting man, I'd wager that it won't happen anytime soon.

It continues to be my personal belief that some of the detractors of BFM do so simply because of their own ineptitude. Other commanders of the past, who were more interested in personal career advancement than the combat skills of their pilots, disdained BFM because of their fear of losing an aircraft (and their careers). Others really do believe that they will always "blow through" the merge, never get tangled up, and **always** let the "magic of technology" do the work. In my opinion, their theory is as flawed as that of a boxer who declares that he will "never hook with a hooker." If you hang around the boxing game long enough, sooner or later you are going to find yourself in that squared ring with the likes of a Joe Frazier. By the same token, if you fly air-to-air combat long enough, one day you will find yourself looking across a turning circle at a guy whose main objective is to see to it that you die for your country. At this point, extending out of the fight is simply not a viable option (unless, of course, you feel that his missile won't run you down). It's like riding a hog... there is no way to get off. It's also a terrible time to learn BFM.

Make no mistake about it, though: I do not advocate BFM as a panacea, but instead as an absolutely essential skill within the professional fighter pilot's stock and trade. Any thoughtful examination of today's aerial combat arena will show that longevity does not accrue to those who make it their habit to enter into sustained turning engagements at the merge. Such action draws enemy fighters like a magnet and makes you highly vulnerable to the unobserved "meat shot." However, great BFM skills will allow you to quickly bring your guns or short-range missiles to bear for the quick kill, while avoiding the pitfalls of the sustained turning fight. They can also ensure that should you find yourself trapped in a 1V1 from which you cannot disengage, that you afford your adversary the opportunity to die for **his** country.

During the course of World War II, the great German ace, Eric Hartmann, shot down at least 352 enemy fighters while using the single employment tactic of SEE, DECIDE, ATTACK and BREAK. Could "Bubi" Hartmann fly great BFM? You bet he could, but unfortunately those most qualified to attest to that fact are no longer here. Yet, he was not single-minded or foolish about the application of his considerable skills. In his book, *The Blonde Knight of Germany*, he details the folly of sole reliance upon sheer "stick and rudder" talent and refers to those so inclined as "Muscle Flyers" (of which, incidentally, there are few, if any, who remain). So if you're looking for a set of baseline employment tactics to adopt, I would suggest that you shamelessly copy that of the "Ace of Aces," for they are as valid in today's best fighters as they were almost a half century ago in the Bf-109. The bottom line is that BFM is to air combat as blocking and tackling are to football. Is it worth your time and effort to master it? I'll close with the following observation:

> Statistics of aerial combat have consistently
> shown that approximately 10% of the fighter
> pilots achieve over 80% of the air-to-air kills.
> Of the thousands of fighter pilots with whom I

have been associated over the years, it has been my good fortune to fly and serve with many of that top 10%. I have never met a single one of them who was not an outstanding BFM pilot. As is said in the accompanying videotape: "In the fighter game, if you can't fly great Basic Fighter Maneuvers, you'll never amount to a hill of beans."

Good hunting and ✔ 6,

Phil "Hands" Handley

Preface

Simply put, the *Art of the Kill* series is a comprehensive audiovisual guide to modern air-to-air combat.

Anyone who enjoys reading "techno-thrillers" describing air combat engagements, who likes watching the popular "Wings" television show, who is interested in the topics of military aviation, air combat or modern flight simulations, and who has wondered how modern jet fighter pilots actually do what they do will enjoy this product. *Art of the Kill* demonstrates the "hows and whys" of modern air combat and is the only product of its kind to present its message in a multimedia format.

The *Art of the Kill* book was written by Pete Bonnani, an Air National Guard officer whose primary job is to train fighter pilots in air-to-air combat. Each chapter in this book begins by describing a situation this Weapons Officer and Instructor Pilot experienced while delivering on-the-ground and in-the-air training to his F-16 pilots. These stories illustrate the complex task of learning modern air combat skills and some of the unusual situations he and his students have experienced in the process.

Most existing books about air-to-air combat are either historical retrospectives, biographies or highly technical texts written primarily as syllabuses for Fighter Weapons training. This is the first study written expressly with the layperson in mind: someone who may find air combat fascinating and may relish the opportunity to understand how it is learned and done, but who has awaited until now an entertaining and understandable treatment of the subject matter.

Immediately following each story in *Art of the Kill* is a series of explanations and diagrams directly relating to the air-to-air combat situation presented in the story and illustrating step-by-step how modern air combat is learned and successfully executed. In addition, for a real "Fighter Weapons School" experience, the lesson plans at the end of the book contain written DLOs for each chapter (a training methodology used in actual Fighter Weapons schools), as well as a brief "quiz" on the material with answer keys.

DLOs – Desired Learning Objectives

Art of the Kill may be read straight through. However, maximum understanding of the air combat experience may best be gained by reading a chapter and then watching the segment in the "Fighter Air Combat Trainer" videotape that accompanies each chapter. This videotape intermixes a presentation on air combat skills with real air combat footage. It also includes historical commentary from retired Colonel Phil "Hands" Handley, a "MiG killer" fighter pilot, who had the only gun kill of a MiG-19 over North Vietnam.

Each segment in "Fighter Air Combat Trainer" is narrated and explained by author Pete Bonanni, and relates the desired objectives of the learning experience by discussing the relevant material. During the explanations, flight simulators and models are used to illustrate both the concepts involved and the actual maneuvers being discussed.

For those who are curious about the flight simulation used in the "Fighter Air Combat Trainer" video, *Art of the Kill* contains a free demonstration disk of *Falcon 3.0*, the most realistic F-16 flight simulation available outside of the military or the aviation industry. With this *Falcon 3.0* demo, those of you who have access to an IBM computer can see for yourselves what air combat is all about, and can actually attempt the maneuvers you have read about in *Art of the Kill* and have seen in "Fighter Air Combat Trainer."

Finally, for those who already have their own copy of *Falcon 3.0*, simulator training missions (called Red Flag Missions after the famous "Red Flag" fighter weapons school run out of Nellis Air Force Base, Nevada) are available for free downloading from the Spectrum HoloByte online bulletin board.

Spectrum HoloByte
Customer Support BBS
510-522-8409
8-N-1

Together, the *Art of the Kill* book, the "Fighter Air Combat Trainer" videotape and the *Falcon 3.0* flight simulator offer a fascinating glimpse into a world few of us have access to: that of the modern fighter pilot and of modern air combat.

Chapter 1

GEOMETRY
OF AIR COMBAT

Overview of Basic Fighter Maneuvers

Basic Fighter Maneuvers or BFM describe how aircraft maneuver against each other in one-versus-one (1V1) air combat. These maneuvers are the basic building blocks of all the other air combat tactics and techniques. You will never achieve true proficiency in any phase of air combat without first understanding BFM.

BFM describes specific concepts of fighter turns, turning room and turn circles. These principles will be discussed in this book in an air-to-air context. Principles of BFM also apply when you're flying air-to-ground missions. A fighter pilot's objective is to kill and survive in the skies over the battlefield.

BFM forms the foundation of the complex skills that a modern fighter pilot must master in order to achieve this objective. From this foundation, we will help you build an in-depth understanding of modern air combat. What you know is important, but in fighter aviation, it is not what you know but how well you achieve your primary objective—a sky full of the enemy's hair, teeth and eyeballs. There are no points for second place. The following story will illustrate this point. *Art of the Kill* will start you on the road to mastering the principles of air combat. Enjoy!

Mud Hens – F-15Es

Not long ago, I had a tussle with some Mud Hens in a Dissimilar Air Combat Tactics (DACT) ride. I was in an F-16, and the bad guys were flying F-15Es. The F-15E is the ground-attack version of the F-15 which flew to fame in the Gulf War, attacking SCUD sites and just about every other kind of target in the theater. The F-15E is a two-seat jet equipped with conformal fuel tanks which increase its range, but limits its maneuverability.

The fight started with a customary "Fight's on" call, and I immediately leaned my two-ship flight of F-16s southwest towards the sun. This move would force the bandits to look into the sun as we got within visual range. We were already outnumbered four to two, so we needed all the help we could get. To make matters worse, we had been briefed that the F-16s would be limited to simulated AIM-9M Sidewinders while the F-15Es would have AIM-7M Sparrows along with their Sidewinders. Because the AIM-7 has a longer range than the AIM-9, we started the fight in the "rope-a-dope" mode. In other words, we could not go right at them because they had the big stick (the AIM-7). When you are up against a fighter with a bigger stick, you have to use deception to keep from getting your cranium creased.

Our game plan for the rope-a-dope was to sort out the Mud Hen formation before we got to Sparrow range. Next, we would determine which one of us was targeted on radar by the F-15Es. If we were both targeted, then we would turn and run. No need to end up wearing a Sparrow. If only one of us was targeted, the targeted jet would drag, and the untargeted Falcon would go to the merge and wring a few Mud Hen necks. In the unlikely event they couldn't find either one of us on radar, we would both go to the merge.

drag – a turn away from the enemy

merge – the point where the opposing fighters pass each other

snot locker – toward my nose

angels 18 – 18,000 feet altitude

Mach – the speed of sound

pucker factor – anxiety level

As the fight unfolded, I got a radar contact on all four bandits. They were in a wall formation coming right down the snot locker. I called to my wingman, "Lead has 4 contacts, 20° left, at angels 18. Wide line abreast formation, high aspect." My wingman called, "Two's same." My wingman and I had all four of them on radar, and we already had some offset. I leaned the flight farther southwest and pushed it up to just below the Mach.

Just after I completed the turn for more offset, my wingman called, "Two is spiked, left 1 o'clock." An F-15E radar had found him. His call was followed by a roll and turn out of the fight. This was our planned maneuver if one of us was found by the F-15Es. With my wingman executing the planned drag, I checked my threat warning again. I knew I would get a tone if I was targeted, but these ears of mine have betrayed me in the past. When the pucker factor is up and the chips are down, only my eyes have proved to be 100% reliable.

Nope, the scope was clean. At 10 miles, I turned to put my targeted F-15E in the HUD. At about eight miles, I picked up a tally and called, "Lead's tally 4, wide line abreast formation." They hadn't seen me, or if they had, they weren't reacting. I closed the range and pressed down on the Z axis of the F-16 cursor slew button. When you press and hold down on the cursor slew button, you switch the Sidewinder from the radar slave mode to the boresight mode. I planned to take out the closest Mud Hen with a boresight Sidewinder shot and then switch to the farthest F-15E in the formation with a radar slave Sidewinder shot. This way I had a chance to kill two guys at the merge and have the other two guys out in front of me. Things were happening at the proper pace, and I was in the groove as I got a good missile tone on the closest Mud Hen. God was in heaven, and the birds were singing in the trees. All was right with the world as I squeezed the trigger in the heart of the Sidewinder envelope. I called, "Fox 2 kill on the southwest Eagle at 18,000 feet."

This is where things got ugly. My shot call on the radio created an explosion of activity in the enemy formation. Suddenly the entire wall of F-15Es turned quickly like a great school of fish and pointed right at me. This move transformed a nice, peaceful wall of Mud Hens into an angry, lead-trail formation. The closest guy flashed past me and aileron rolled to signal he knew he was dead. The rest of the formation was very much alive and aware that there was a Falcon in their knickers. I tried to uncage the Sidewinder on the trail F-15E, but the sky was full of flares, including my own.

"Crap, what do I do now?" I thought to myself. I couldn't kill the trail F-15 as planned. My game plan unraveled, causing the clear mind of one of America's killer elite to turn to mush. This clear, calculating mind was quickly replaced by the bane of all fighter pilots— the "random thought generator." A stupid idea that sprung unbidden in the confusion was "gun the trailer." That was all I could think of. "Gun the trailer—yeah, it might work." In response to this neural spasm, I laid 8 Gs on the jet and squared a corner that was practically unsquarable. When I started the turn, I was at 90° of aspect, at a range of 4,000 feet from the F-15E. I ended up right in the heart of the gun envelope and quickly tracked the trailing Mud Hen. The guy reacted like he was struck on the head with a board. While my turn surprised me, it must have mesmerized the target because he never even jinked out of plane. He just kept pulling into me and gave me an easy shot.

I called, "Tracking kill on the F-15E at 17,000 feet, nose low, passing through west." It was now a 2V1 fight. "Now, where the hell are those other Mud Hens?" I rolled to do a belly check and picked up a tally at 8 o'clock level. The two Mud Hens were nose on at 6,000 feet. Not too bad—I could do a high G bat turn, pass them head-on and separate. I rolled to put my lift vector on them and started to pull. Nothing. The nose would not move. My mind started to clear as I realized that I had just taken a 450 knot fighting machine and turned it into a 150 knot grape that was about to get eaten. I had two options—both of them lethal. Extend to get energy and soak up a missile, or try to turn the jet with no airspeed and get gunned. Neither choice was good, but fighter pilot instinct took over, and I turned into the closest Mud Hen. The fight ended (but not until I performed a feeble jink out).

jink out – defensive maneuver against a gun attack

What went wrong? I did everything correctly up until the moment I committed to a 3V1 turning fight. The F-15E is the best air-to-ground fighter in the world. It is also a very respectable air-to-air jet and is very similar in performance to a Turkey. It is no match, however, for an F-16 in a maneuvering fight. I got shot because of pure buffoonery. Many fights come down to the ability of the pilot to maneuver his jet in a 1V1 situation. In this fight with the Mud Hens, I should have realized the position of my escape window and separated (a concept we will discuss in Chapter 4). In addition, I used up far more energy than necessary turning on the trailing bandit. BFM is the first critical set of skills that a fighter pilot must learn. In this case, I flew my BFM like a plumber, not a fighter pilot, and paid the price.

Turkey – F-14

Introduction to the Geometry of Air Combat

When I was a pimply-faced Cadet at the Air Force Academy, I had an Aeronautical Engineering professor that we all called Captain Sominex. Captain Sominex could take the most motivated and dedicated student and within minutes turn him into a slobbering, head-bobbing imbecile, fighting a losing battle to stay coherent. You can imagine his effect on a student like myself with a somewhat more casual approach to academic life at the Zoo (that's what the cadets called the Air Force Academy). In fact, I still have the scars on my forehead (now covered by wrinkles) from my head banging off the desk. All of this did not faze the Captain, however; he just continued to drone on about Bernoulli's Equations and the Law of Continuity as waves of heads bobbed and drooled, almost marking time to his writing on the board. The funny thing about old Captain Sominex's Aero class, though, is that it is one of the few subjects that I had at the Zoo that I still use today. I obviously don't have to solve aero problems, but it does help to understand how jets fly and how engines push air out the back.

Well, the same thing can be said for this chapter on geometry. It may not be the most exciting section in *Art of the Kill*; however, it isn't possible to discuss air combat if we don't know the terms and definitions used to describe the spatial relationship between two aircraft. Further, just like my Aero courses, you'll find you'll use the information in this section long after you finish reading the book.

Now, in order to perform BFM, a fighter pilot must understand his spatial relationship to the target from three perspectives: positional geometry, attack geometry and the weapons envelope. Like any profession, air combat has several unique terms that are a necessary part of the language.

Positional Geometry

Angle-off, range and aspect angle are terms used in BFM discussions to describe the relative advantage or disadvantage that one aircraft has in relation to another.

Angle-off

Angle-off is the difference, measured in degrees, between your heading and the bandit's. This angle provides information about the relative fuselage alignment between the pilot's jet and the bandit's. For example, if the angle-off between you and a bandit were 0°, you would be on a parallel heading with the bandit, and the two fuselages would be aligned. If the angle-off were 90°, your fuselage would be perpendicular to the bandit. Angle-off is also called Heading Crossing Angle or HCA. Figure 1-1 shows angle-off.

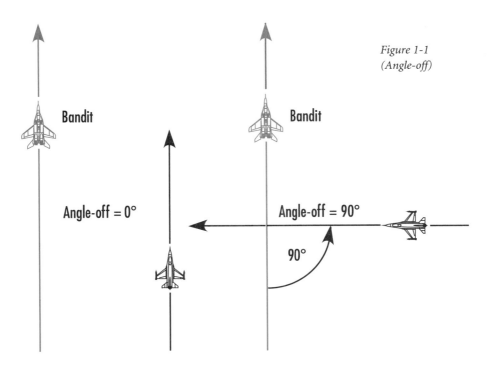

Figure 1-1
(Angle-off)

Bandit

Bandit

Angle-off = 0°

Angle-off = 90°

90°

Range

HUDs –
Head-Up Displays

Range is the distance between your jet and the bandit. In most HUDs, range is measured in feet, out to one nautical mile (6,000 feet). Outside one nautical mile, range is measured in miles and tenths of miles. For example, a range to the target of 9,000 feet would be displayed as 1.5 nautical miles. Figure 1-2 shows range.

Figure 1-2
(Range)

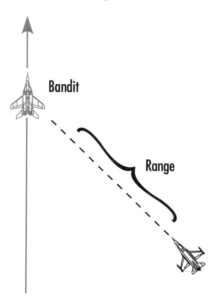

Aspect Angle

Aspect angle is the number of degrees measured from the tail of a target to your aircraft. Aspect angle is important because it indicates how far away your aircraft is from the target's 6 o'clock position. Aspect angle has nothing to do with your heading, as is shown in Figure 1-3. Note that the aspect angle stays the same, regardless of which way your aircraft is heading. Along with a measure in degrees from the target's tail, Figure 1-3 describes aspect angle as either right or left. In order to determine if the angle is left or right aspect, start at the target's 6 o'clock facing the target. If your aircraft is in the right hemisphere, you have right aspect; in the left hemisphere, you have left target aspect. Aspect angle is important because, if you know the aspect angle and range to the target, you then know his lateral displacement or turning room from the target—and lateral displacement is very important in BFM.

Figure 1-3
(Aspect Angle)

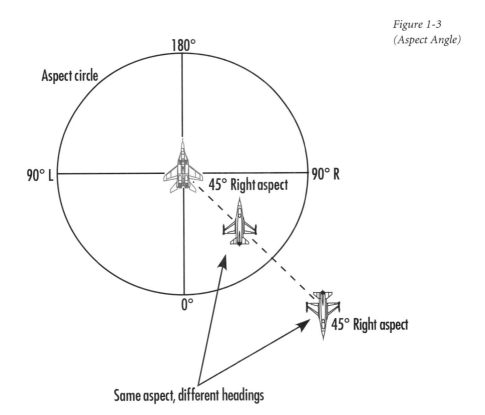

Same aspect, different headings

Attack Geometry

Attack geometry describes the path that the offensive fighter takes as he converges on the bandit. When you start an attack on the bandit, there are three distinct paths or pursuit courses you can follow. These pursuit courses are lag pursuit, pure pursuit and lead pursuit. If you are pointing your aircraft behind the bandit, you are in lag pursuit. If you are pointing directly at the bandit, you are in pure pursuit. If you are pointing in front of the bandit, you are in lead pursuit. Figure 1-4 shows the pursuit options that can be taken by the attacking fighter.

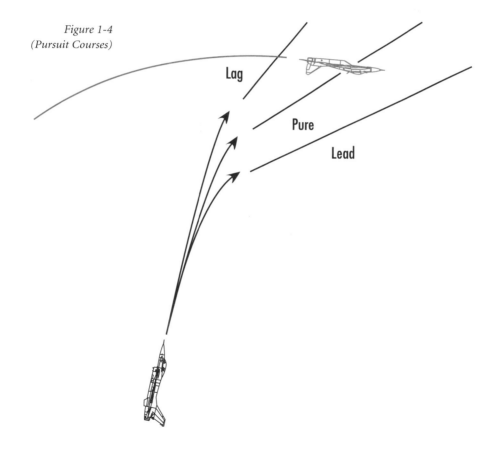

Figure 1-4
(Pursuit Courses)

Lag

Pure

Lead

Lag Pursuit

Lag pursuit is used primarily on the approach to the bandit. Lag is also used any time an attacking fighter maneuvers out of plane (that is, not in the same plane of motion as the fighter under attack). You must have the ability to out-turn the bandit in order to fly lag pursuit for any length of time. The reason? In order to shoot a missile or the gun at the enemy, you must pull your nose out of lag. If the bandit can turn at a higher rate, he can keep your nose stuck in lag and keep you from shooting him.

Pure Pursuit

Pure pursuit is used to shoot *missiles* at the enemy. Flying a pure pursuit course all the way into the bandit will lead to an overshoot. For this reason, you should only point at the bandit when you are going to shoot. Figure 1-5 shows how holding a pure pursuit course will lead to an overshoot.

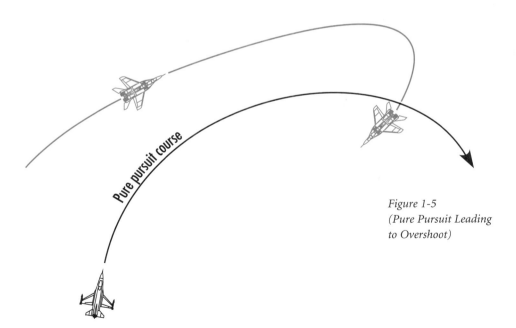

*Figure 1-5
(Pure Pursuit Leading
to Overshoot)*

Lead Pursuit

Lead pursuit is used to close on the bandit and is also used for *gun shots*. Flying a lead pursuit course is the fastest way to get to the bandit because you cut him off in the sky. The problem with establishing a lead pursuit course too early is that you will overshoot the bandit when you get in close unless you have a significant turn rate advantage. If you are fighting a similar aircraft, such as the MiG-29, you will not normally be able to stay in lead and will be forced into an overshoot, similar to the one depicted in Figure 1-5. It is important, however, to establish lead pursuit at the proper time in the fight because it is the only way that you can get into the gun envelope.

Determining the Pursuit Course

If the attacker is in the defender's plane of motion, the velocity vector of the attacker determines the pursuit

Figure 1-6
(Falcon HUD with
Flight Path Marker)

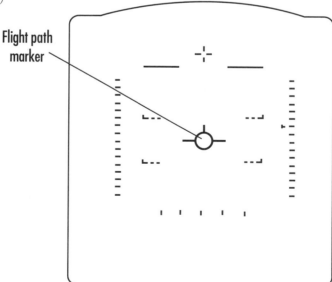

Flight path marker

course. The velocity vector, for the sake of our discussion, is the nose of the aircraft and represents the direction that your jet travels through the air at any given time. From the cockpit, the velocity vector is depicted by the flight path marker. Figure 1-4 shows a case where the attacker and defender are in the same plane of motion. Figure 1-6 shows an F-16 flight path marker.

What if the attacker is not in the same plane of motion as the defender? How do you determine the pursuit course for out-of-plane maneuvering? When the attacker is not in the same plane as the defender, pursuit course is determined by the lift vector of the attacker. An aircraft's lift vector is simply a vector that sticks directly out of the top of the jet, perpendicular to the aircraft's wings. At high G, an aircraft moves along its lift vector. You position the lift vector by rolling, and when you pull Gs, the nose of the jet tracks toward the lift vector. Figure 1-7 shows a fighter's lift vector.

Figure 1-7
(Lift Vector)

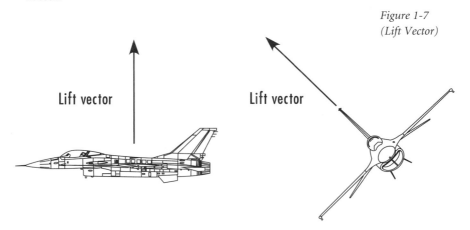

Lift vector   Lift vector

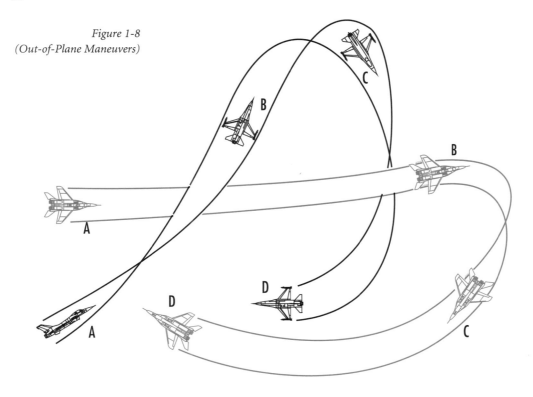

Figure 1-8
(Out-of-Plane Maneuvers)

If an attacker pulls out of plane with a bandit, his pursuit course is then determined by where his lift vector is taking him. When the attacker pulls out of plane with a bandit, he is, by definition, flying lag pursuit. As he pulls back into a bandit, he may be flying lag, pure or lead pursuit, depending on the geometry of the fight. Figure 1-8 shows an F-16 pulling out of plane with a MiG-29. (This figure does not show a recommended maneuver but rather illustrates the effect of out-of-plane maneuvering on the pursuit course.)

In this figure, the F-16 immediately goes to lag pursuit when he pulls his nose out of plane in position B. At the top of this maneuver, he initiates a pull back down into the defender at position C. In this position, the F-16 is in pure pursuit. Notice at position D, when the F-16 enters the

MiG-29's plane-of-motion, his nose is on the Fulcrum and he is again flying a pure pursuit course.

Where you position the nose of the aircraft is very important when a pilot attacks the bandit. In the next chapter, "Offensive BFM," the *use* of attack pursuit geometry will be explained in detail, and we will talk in specific terms about where to place the jet in relationship to the bandit. For now, just make sure you understand what each of the pursuit courses are and what they do for you.

The Weapons Envelope

The weapons envelope is the area around the bandit where your missiles or gun can be effective. The weapons envelope is defined by angle-off, range and aspect angle. The dimensions and position of this area are dictated by the type of weapons you are carrying.

If your jet is loaded with all-aspect AIM-9Ms or AIM-120s missiles, the area around the bandit looks like a doughnut; the outside ring being maximum range (Rmax) and the inside ring being minimum range (Rmin). Figure 1-9 shows a shaded doughnut area which represents an all-aspect missile engagement zone. With each missile, Rmax and Rmin are different. Generally speaking, missiles that have a greater range or Rmax also have a greater minimum range or Rmin.

*Figure 1-9
(All-Aspect Missile
Engagement Zone)*

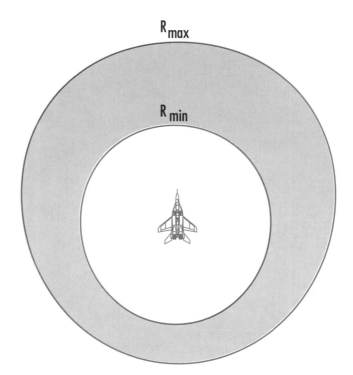

Notice the oval shape of the all-aspect missile envelope. More of the area is in front of the bandit than behind him because a missile fired at high aspect on a bandit (that is, from in front), has a greater *effective range* than a missile fired at low-aspect (from behind). If you shoot a missile head-on at a bandit, the mere fact that the bandit is flying towards you will help the missile reach its target. The missile may actually fly a shorter distance to hit the bandit head-on than if it were fired at the bandit's six. However, the range at which you first launch the missile will be greater, and this is what is important. The farther away you can launch a missile on the bandit and still have that missile be effective, the better. Always strive to get maximum performance out of your weapons. Another way to increase a missile's effective range is to launch at a significantly higher altitude than the bandit. This will give your missile a reserve of potential energy that it can convert into kinetic energy.

Figure 1-9 shows a target at 1 G. As a target pulls Gs, the weapons envelope shifts. Generally, the limits of Rmax and Rmin in front of the aircraft both move out in the direction of the turn, while Rmax and Rmin behind the aircraft move in on the belly side of turn. Figure 1-10 shows a target in a 5 G turn. The important point to remember is that a bandit that is in fear of dying will turn into you at high G. When this happens, Rmin expands outward from the target at a rapid rate, and within seconds you may be inside minimum range for a missile shot.

*Figure 1-10
(Missile Engagement
Zone at 5 Gs)*

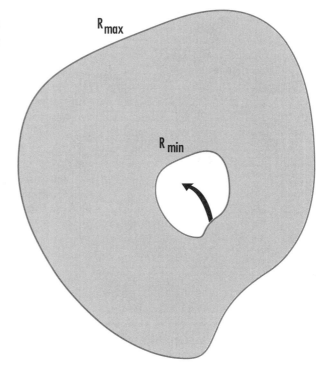

For Guns

The gun is different from missiles in that it has no minimum range. The gun weapons envelope is a circle around the bandit depicting the gun's maximum range. There is no minimum range circle. Figure 1-11 shows the gun envelope.

Remember, a fighter pilot must be aware of where he is at all times in respect to his weapons envelope.

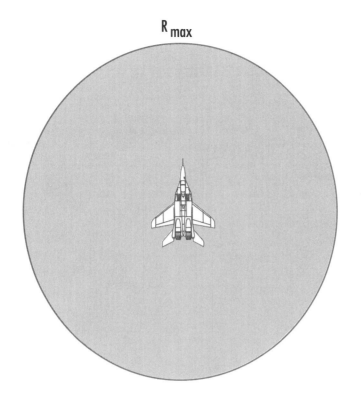

R **max**

*Figure 1-11
(Gun Envelope)*

Conclusion

The geometry of the fight is important. Before we move on, you should understand the terms and definitions covered in this section. The academic lecture on the videotape will reinforce your knowledge of BFM geometry. After viewing the first section of the tape, you can take the quiz on BFM geometry located in "BFM Lesson Plans."

Chapter 2

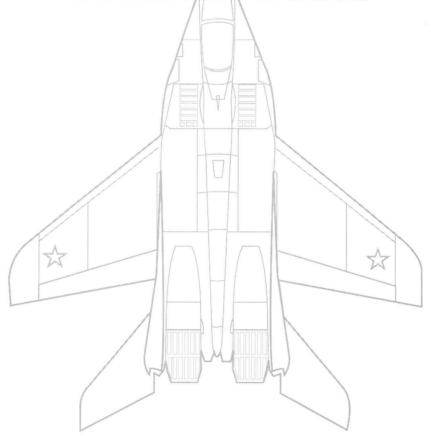

OFFENSIVE BFM

Offensive BFM

It was a great fall day at MacDill AFB in Tampa, Florida. I was flying a BFM ride with the "Top Dogs"— the 61st Fighter Squadron. This was my seventh ride in the F-16C, and I was quickly learning to love the power of that big GE engine and the improved avionics. My previous 850 hours in the F-16 had been in A models, which are much lighter (and more primitive) than the C model. The A model is powered by the old version of the Pratt and Whitney F100, which was a good engine when it was made, but is an underpowered relic compared to the GE F101 that powers the Block 30 F-16 flown by the 61st. Even my memory of the Pratt-powered F-16A had faded somewhat, however, because my most recent 500 hours of fighter time had been in the venerable A-7D Corsair II.

I had left MacDill AFB and the F-16A five years earlier for A-7D training out in Tucson, Arizona. My Guard squadron expected to fly the A-7 for a year or two after I arrived and then make the transition to F-16s. That "year or two" turned into five years of doing nothing but flying low and bombing, bombing and more bombing. Not that I have anything against bombing, mind you. It's just that when all you do is bomb, it gets old fast, especially if you're a former Viper driver. We did do something that we *called* air-to-air in the A-7, but fighting air-to-air in an A-7 is like watching bowling on TV—it's slow and boring. You come into the fight at about 400 knots and quickly get slower and lower. Nobody has any energy to maneuver after about 90° of turn, and it's impossible to get any energy back without extending for several minutes. Most fights end up in a kind of neutral wallow. Year after year of this type of air-to-air had atrophied my BFM skills to the point that I was starting to have trouble keeping my hands from banging into each other when I was debriefing a BFM fight. (I also could only chew gum while sitting down for fear of seriously injuring myself.)

But now, it was five years later, and I was very happy to be back driving an F-16 in the skies over sunny Florida. Taxiing out to fly, I still looked the part—shock of unruly hair hanging down from the front of my helmet, boyish grin on my face, piercing gaze. It's too bad looks are irrelevant in fighters. The only thing that counts is what's inside. My cranium was crammed with all the correct terms and techniques of F-16 BFM, but it remained to be seen whether or not any of this would come out once good old American aluminum started to strain under a G load.

perch setups – setups in front of the attacker

In the F-16C syllabus, this ride was called BFM-1. BFM-1 consists of offensive perch setups starting from 3,000 feet and working out to 9,000 feet. The 3,000-foot setup is essentially a gun fight with both fighters starting at 300 knots. At the "Fight's on" call, the instructor pilot (IP), from a position out in front, does some serious moves to stay alive while the student (yours truly) tries to film him under the gun sight.

In this case, the IP was a blond-haired guy that we called "Poster Child." At the "Fight's on" call, he initiated an 8 G break, slightly out of plane. The fight started with my jet slightly to the inside of the turn, so as the IP made his move, I leaned to lag for a couple of seconds and then started to pull back to lead pursuit. Within another two seconds, I realized that I was in lag for too long because I could not get my nose on the IP as he started to pull slightly nose high. I was stuck in lag as the fight started uphill. Poster Child kept a tally

crawl back up into the cockpit – mentally catch up with the aircraft

throughout the fight and quickly called "knock it off." Wow! This was happening fast. The whole fight lasted less than 10 seconds. I was so far behind in this fight that I felt like I was hanging on the tail of the jet. We set up again, and I got back on a 3,000 foot perch. I decided I better crawl back up into the cockpit, or I would never shoot this guy.

The next fight started the same way, but this time, I only leaned toward lag for a split second and then went right to lead pursuit. In a gun fight, you know you're going to win when you see your opponent make an aggressive out-of-plane maneuver to keep from getting shot. When I first went to lead pursuit, I pulled the throttle out of burner to slow my overtake. As I entered the gun envelope with my airspeed under control,

Poster Child knew that he could not stick me in lag or get me to overshoot so he started to jink out of plane. I had him. I got a good shot and called a kill, ending the fight.

On the next setup, I started back at 6,000 feet. The 6,000 foot setup is the easiest offensive perch position to start from because you're just outside the bandit's turn circle. (The chapter you're about to read covers all of this turn circle stuff.) On this fight, Poster Child started a very high-G defensive turn straight into me, but I flew textbook offense and quickly got into guns parameters. As I approached the guns positions, my eyes beheld a sight I hadn't seen before. Poster Child reversed the direction of his turn as I approached him and started pulling away from me instead of executing a classic jink out of plane. As I started to reposition, he again reversed his turn direction and started to pull away from me.

I was getting confused as I closed the range, so I did what I always do when I'm confused and flying guns offensive—I set my wings to the horizon and pulled up away from the bandit. As soon as I was established in the vertical, I rolled back to watch what he was doing. This move kept me from overshooting at close range and slowed the pace of the fight. After pulling in the vertical and rolling back to keep a tally on Poster Child, I noticed he was *real* slow, and his speed brakes were extended. Poster Child's jet looked like it was hanging from a string, though in reality, he still had about 120 knots of airspeed. No problem. I kept the nose up, and after I had bled off a few more knots, I started back down into him. He had given up all his energy (maneuvering potential) to spit me out, and he was a goner when I didn't blow past him. This fight ended with me in the saddle as both of our jets hung on the burner at very high alpha.

alpha – angle of attack

I really didn't know what the heck he was doing during that guns defense until Poster Child described it later in the debrief. It turned out that the maneuver he executed was called the "snake defense." In Chapter 3, we'll discuss how to use this move to keep from getting gunned. In order for it to work, a guy must try to follow you through it. I didn't follow him in this fight. When I saw the move unfold, I pulled away. The maneuver turned out to a good counter to a snake guns defense.

Well, the fun didn't end there. The next setup was from 9,000 feet. On a 9,000 foot perch, you're well outside the bandit's turn circle, so you have to know (and execute) more BFM to get into a guns position. This fight started well as I drove into the turn circle and initiated my first turn. As I kept pulling toward Poster Child at about 7 Gs, however, things started to go bad. I kept pulling into Poster Child as he executed a "continuous turn" defense with his lift vector right on me. My turn rate, of course, was better than his at this point because he had turned for a longer period of time and had bled off more airspeed. His turn radius, however, was tighter (also due to his lower airspeed). As the fight continued, I used my superior turn rate to pull my nose toward his jet. But as I pulled his jet into the HUD, something didn't look right.

"What the heck is wrong?"

The range between the jets closed, and the pace of the fight quickened. Poster Child was in the HUD, but the line-of-sight rate was too great. Things were happening fast when suddenly a "helmet fire" broke out in my cockpit. A helmet fire—also known as a "cranium melt-down"—causes a fighter pilot's brain to experience a kind of rapid reverse evolution. In this state, you try to attack and kill whatever is in your field of view at the time, regardless of the consequences. Luckily, Poster

Child was still out in front me, so in a blur of rapid events that didn't "feel" right, I went for guns. I missed and then grossly overshot to the outside of the turn. Poster Child immediately reversed his turn, and there I was, helmet on fire in a flat scissors. After a few slow turns in the scissors, it was clear that neither side was going to get the advantage, so Poster Child called "knock it off" and ended the fight. After this fight, we had both reached bingo, so we rejoined for a battle damage check and then headed back to MacDill.

The only real trouble I had during BFM-1 was with the 9,000 foot setup. After drawing it out on the grease board back in the squadron room, I understood why. You cannot stay in a constant high-G turn against a continuously turning bandit when starting from 9,000 feet. If you do, you'll end up with a very high-angle gun shot at endgame. At some point in the fight, you must ease off the G, drive back farther into lag, and get closer to the bandit before going to lead pursuit. Chapter 2, "Offensive BFM," will reveal several such important air combat tenets. You'll learn not just what to do (like easing off the G after your initial turn on a 9,000-foot perch), but why these techniques work.

Introduction to Offensive BFM

The ultimate goal of offensive BFM is to kill the bandit in the minimum amount of time. In order to accomplish this goal, the fighter pilot must understand basic offensive maneuvering. It is helpful to think of offensive BFM as a series of fluid rolls, turns and accelerations. Some of the maneuvers in offensive BFM have names, but the modern day fighter pilot thinks in terms of driving his jet into the control position from an offensive setup, rather than in terms of executing a series of named "moves" to counter the bandit's defensive maneuvering. The sustained maneuverability of a modern fighter has made a "move–counter-move" discussion of offensive BFM obsolete. This study guide reflects current offensive BFM thinking.

It may seem obvious, but the primary reason that you need offensive BFM techniques is to counter a bandit's turn. When you are behind a bandit who is flying straight and level, it is a simple matter to control your airspeed with the throttle and fly around behind him. When the bandit turns, however, things change dramatically. A turning bandit will immediately create BFM problems as shown in Figure 2-1.

Figure 2-1
(BFM Problems)

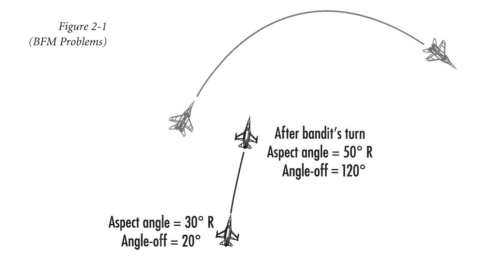

After bandit's turn
Aspect angle = 50° R
Angle-off = 120°

Aspect angle = 30° R
Angle-off = 20°

In order to stay in weapons parameters and in control of the bandit, you must stay at his 6 o'clock. To do this, you must maintain control of angle-off, range and aspect angle. Remember from Chapter 1 that these terms defined the angular relationship between two aircraft. Figure 2-1 shows how a bandit's turn will change the angular relationship between the offensive and defensive fighter. To control the "angles" and stay at 6 o'clock, the offensive fighter must also turn his jet. Figure 2-2 shows why an immediate turn by the offensive fighter will not work. If the offensive fighter goes into a turn to match the defensive fighter, he will just end up out in front because the center of their turn circles are offset.

Figure 2-2
(Immediate Turn =
Overshoot)

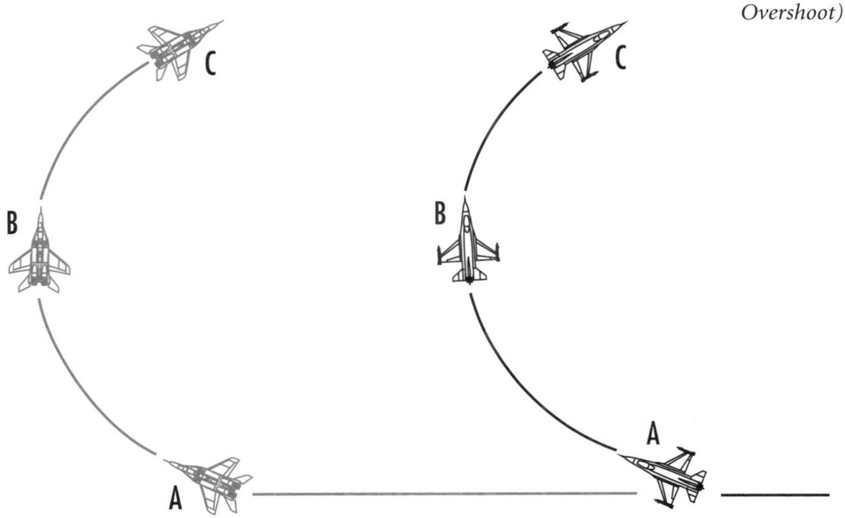

An immediate turn will not work, and driving straight will not work. A turn of some sort is the solution to solving the BFM problems of angle-off, aspect angle and range caused by the bandit's defensive turn. The problem is twofold— how to turn and when to turn. Let's look first at the mechanics of turns.

BFM and Turns

BFM has a lot to do with turns. It is important to understand several concepts about turns in order to be successful at BFM. These include the concepts of positional energy, turn radius, turn rate, corner velocity and vertical turns.

Power for Position

"P_s (specific power) for position" is a concept that is an integral part of BFM. Fighters have two types of energy: kinetic and potential. Kinetic energy is simply the velocity or speed at which the jet is traveling. Potential energy is "stored" energy that can be converted to kinetic energy. Potential energy is directly related to aircraft altitude. If a jet is at high altitude, its potential energy is high. If the same jet is flying at low altitude, its potential energy is low. *Always remember that you can trade altitude (potential energy) for speed.* Likewise, you can convert aircraft speed back into altitude or potential energy.

You can also exchange energy for nose position. Anytime you maneuver or turn a fighter, it "costs" energy. When you turn a jet at high G, you "spend" or lose energy. That's the bad news. The good news is that the defensive fighter also gives up energy to turn and defend himself.

Turn Radius and Turn Rate

The math involved to calculate turn radius is:
TR (turn radius) = V^2/gG
V is the aircraft's velocity in feet per second. Little g is gravity, and big G is the G the aircraft is pulling.

The first two characteristics of turns are turn radius and turn rate. Turn radius is simply a measure of how tight your jet is turning. If you are looking down on the aircraft as it turns, the turn radius is the distance from the center of your turn circle to the aircraft, measured in feet.

It is not important that you understand how to compute turn radius. Just realize that velocity is squared in the turn radius equation, meaning that turn radius will grow exponentially based on velocity. The equation also includes aircraft Gs. The more Gs that you pull, the tighter the turn. Still, velocity is squared, **so airspeed has a greater effect on turn radius than G.**

Turn rate is the second important factor for turning the jet. Turn rate indicates how fast the aircraft moves around the turn radius or circle we just talked about. It is also described as how fast an aircraft can change its nose position. Turn rate is measured in degrees per second and is also dependent on Gs and airspeed.

Turn rate = K G/V
K is a constant and big G and V are the same as in the equation for turn radius.

The higher the G in the above equation, the faster the turn rate. Velocity still remains an important factor. Notice that G is divided by velocity. If G remains at maximum, a higher velocity will cause turn rate to decrease. The reverse is true: a lower velocity will yield a higher turn rate.

Corner Velocity

You may think that slowing down to minimum airspeed and pulling as hard as you can is the best course of action in order to achieve a high turn rate. Not so fast. There is a relationship between airspeed and Gs. At lower airspeeds, you have less G available or, in other words, you can't pull as many Gs as you get slow. Less lift is produced by the wings of an aircraft at slower speeds, and as a result, there is less force available to turn the aircraft. If you get going really fast (above Mach 1, for example), you also lose G availability. For every fighter, there is an optimum airspeed for achieving the highest turn rate. The airspeed where the jet has the quickest turn rate with the smallest turn radius is called corner velocity. In most modern fighters, it is between 400 to 500 KCAS. The F-16 has a corner velocity of about 450 KCAS.

KCAS – knots, computed airspeed

Figure 2-3 shows the relationship between airspeed (labeled as a Mach number), turn rate and turn radius. The top of the figure shows turn rate and turn radius broken out individually, while the bottom of the graph shows them combined. These graphs in Figure 2-3 are generic turn rate and radius charts. The bottom chart represents the approximate turn performance of an F-16.

Figure 2-3 (Turn Rate and Radius Charts)

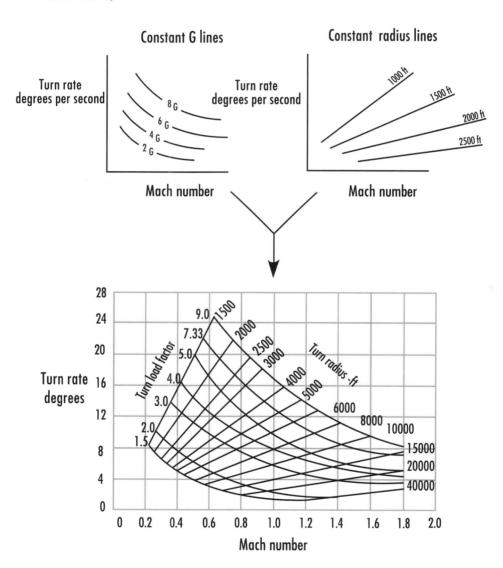

Note that at 0.6 Mach, the jet can pull 9 Gs and turn at a rate of 24° per second. At 0.6 Mach, the jet can also turn in a radius of 1,500 feet. This is the best (tightest) radius the jet can achieve at the highest turn rate possible. The jet can turn this same radius at slower airspeeds, but turn rate will go down significantly. At 0.4 Mach, for example, the jet can turn with a radius of 1,500 feet, but the turn rate falls from 24° to 16° a second. Just to put this figure in perspective, a 2° per second turn rate advantage will allow you to dominate an adversary.

The airspeed of a jet can be controlled by the pilot in the following four ways:

▶ Throttle position

▶ Drag devices

▶ Nose position in relation to the horizon

▶ Aircraft G

Throttle position controls how much slow, cold air you turn into fast, hot gas. Drag devices refer primarily to speed brakes. Nose position in relation to the horizon also affects airspeed. For example, a nose-low position will increase your airspeed because of the effect of gravity. Finally, G force causes airspeed to bleed off. Remember the brief discussion earlier about exchanging energy for position. No modern fighter flying at medium altitude can stay at corner velocity while pulling max Gs for long. As you pull Gs, you will get slower. It is important, however, to start maneuvering close to corner velocity because the first turn you make is usually the most important in the fight.

Fighter pilots should think in terms of both turn rate and turn radius. A fighter with a superior turn rate can outmaneuver a fighter that has a poor turn rate but a tighter turn radius. Fighter pilots have a simple two-word saying: "Rate kills." What this means is that the ability to move (or rate) your nose is the primary means of employing weapons (which is what offensive BFM is all about). A bandit may have a tight turn circle, but if you can rate your nose on him and shoot, the fight is over. The flaming wreckage will no longer cause you BFM problems.

Vertical Turns

I have heard it said (incorrectly) that you fly in relation to the bandit and not the earth. While it is obvious that you must fly in relation to the bandit, you must simultaneously keep your nose in control of the horizon. Gravity affects airspeed, as already mentioned. Gravity also affects G availability. If you pull the nose of a fighter straight across the horizon, gravity will have no effect on your turn performance. When you pull the nose up or down, however, gravity becomes a player.

Figure 2-4 introduces a new term: radial G. To understand how an aircraft turns, you must understand that there are two factors that determine the rate and radius of a fighter's turn. The first is the G being felt and read out on the G meter in the cockpit. The second is the pull of gravity. Radial G is a term used by fighter pilots to describe the effective G that determines a fighter's turn. Figure 2-4 shows this concept by depicting a fighter doing a loop. In Figure 2-4, the cockpit G (the G felt by the pilot) is a constant 5 Gs. You will notice that when an aircraft is straight and level and trying to pull in the vertical, the effective G or radial G is only 4. Gravity is subtracted from cockpit G so that the jet is pulling only 4 radial Gs. When the fighter is pulling 5 Gs in the cockpit in the pure vertical (90° point) either straight up or straight down, gravity has no effect, so radial G is equal to cockpit G. When the fighter is inverted and pulling straight down at 5 Gs, gravity adds 1 G to your effective or radial G. The fighter, in effect, is turning at 6 Gs at this point. Radial G then is simply a term that describes the effective or turning G created by combining the positive or negative influence of gravity with cockpit G.

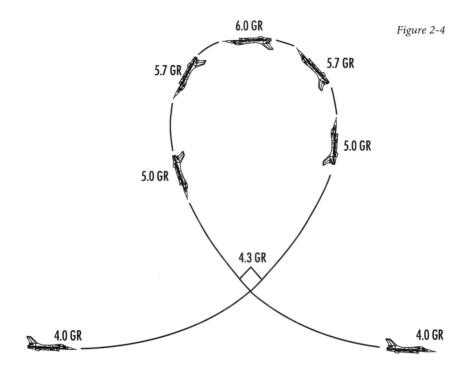

Figure 2-4

What Figure 2-4 shows is that cockpit G is not equal to radial or turning G when maneuvering in the vertical. Remember that 2° per second is a significant turning advantage. The extra G you can get by placing your nose below the horizon when you turn can give you at least 2° per second turn advantage. Most of the time, 1 GR equates to 3°–4° per second.

The concept of radial G can be seen in Figure 2-5. In this figure, both fighters are pulling the same cockpit G. Notice that the fighter with his lift vector below the horizon is turning tighter. What is not so obvious in this figure is that the fighter turning toward the ground is also moving or rating the nose faster.

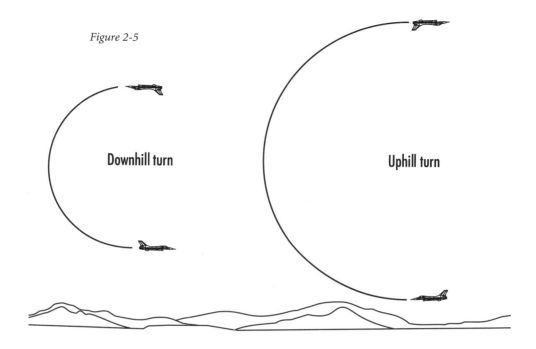

Figure 2-5

Downhill turn

Uphill turn

Turning Room

When a bandit turns his jet, he creates BFM problems for you. To solve these problems, you need to turn *your* jet. In order to turn your jet and solve these BFM problems, you need turning room. Turning room is the offset or distance from the bandit. There are three basic types of turning room: lateral (or horizontal) turning room, vertical turning room, and a combination of both. In order to understand the concept of turning room, you must first understand turn circles. Turn circles are simply the paths that a fighter cuts through the sky when it turns. Figure 2-6 shows a turn circle.

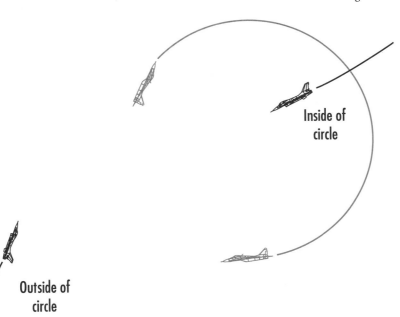

Figure 2-6

Inside of circle

Outside of circle

The concept of turn circles is critically important to understand because, in order to turn and solve BFM problems created by the bandit, you must first drive your jet inside the bandit's turn circle.

Here's how turn circles and turning room are related.

A bandit turns his jet to defend against your attack. You need to get displacement from the bandit in the horizontal or vertical in order to turn and stay behind him. If you try to get displacement while you are still outside the bandit's turn circle, it will not work. Why? Because if you are outside the bandit's turn circle, the bandit can get around the turn and meet you close to head-on. This means that the bandit can turn and take away your turning room. Figure 2-7 shows a fighter turning for lateral offset outside a defender's turn circle.

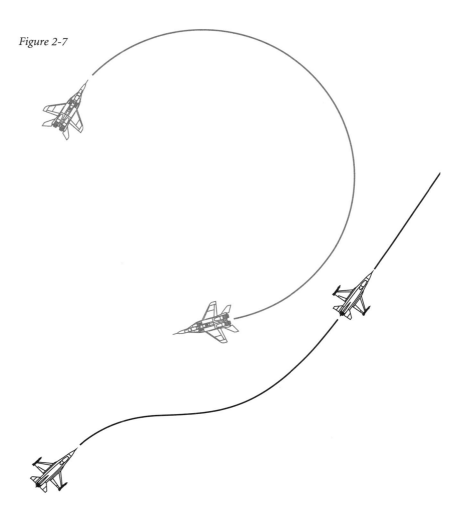

Figure 2-7

The bandit just keeps pulling, leaving the defender with no turning room. This same principle also works in the vertical. Figure 2-8 shows a fighter climbing, doing an old maneuver called a "high yo-yo."

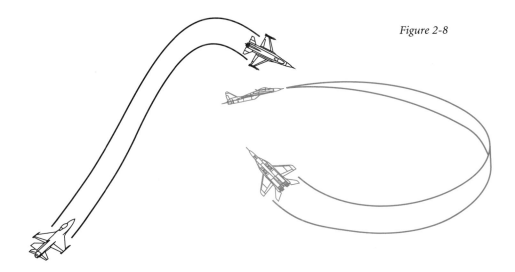

Figure 2-8

It is very dangerous to try to get turning room in the vertical, outside the bandit's turn circle. If you are climbing in the vertical outside or close to the bandit's turn circle, the bandit can get his nose around on you. When you pass at high aspect, the bandit will be nose high while you will be nose low. The bandit gets the first use of gravity to increase his radial G as you pass and will probably get behind you. For this reason, do not try to get turning room outside the bandit's turn circle.

Any maneuvering you do outside the bandit's turn circle will delay you from getting inside the bandit's turn circle. You must be inside the bandit's turn circle in order to turn and solve the BFM problem. In the next section, we will describe how to determine if you are inside or outside the turn circle of the bandit and how to use BFM to get and stay in weapons parameters.

Solving the Offensive BFM Problem

The reason you are out there burning jet fuel is simple: to get into weapons parameters and shoot. BFM is real simple against a guy hanging in a chute. All you have to do is watch out for him shooting at you with his pistol as you fly by and wave. Anytime you can take a shot and end the fight, do it. The problem is that when you start from 1.0 to 1.5 nm behind the bandit and he turns, you will only be in AIM-9M parameters for a very short time. The AIM-9M is just like every other heat missile out there today—it doesn't like the high line-of-sight rates generated by targets in tight, turning fights. You have time for one shot. If you miss, you had better be ready to put some offensive BFM on him, or you will end up wearing an AA-11 Archer. The end result of your best offensive BFM will be a gun shot. Here is how you do it.

The bandit turns. The first question you must ask yourself is "Am I inside or outside the bandit's turn circle?"

How do you know? Watch the bandit's turn.

If the bandit's present turn rate will force his nose on you or even close to you, you are outside the bandit's turn circle. For modern fighters at high G, you are normally outside the bandit's turn circle at ranges outside 2 nm. At 1 nm, you are normally inside the bandit's turn circle, and between these ranges, you are in a transition zone. These ranges, of course, do not really matter to a fighter pilot. When you start behind a bandit, you simply fight what you see. As the bandit turns, you predict where he is going and maneuver based on this prediction. For example, if the bandit is only pulling 4 Gs, then at 2 nm you are still inside his turn circle. Figure 2-9 shows the difference between starting at 2 nm from a 4 G target and starting at 2 nm from a 7 G target.

nm – nautical miles

Figure 2-9

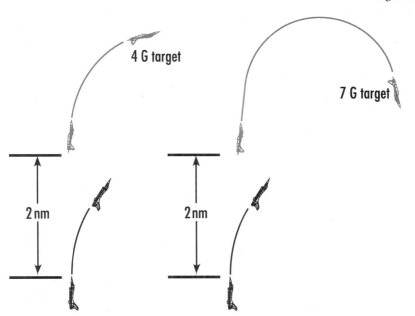

Most fighter pilots will not pull only 4 Gs, however, when they are in danger of dying. Still, you fight what you see.

If you are outside the bandit's turn circle at the beginning of the fight, you are not in an offensive fight—you are in a head-on BFM fight. Head-on BFM is the subject of Chapter 4, but for now, just think about an AIM-9M shot in this situation. The bandit cannot shoot you until he gets his nose around to within about 40° of your jet. You should be able to get one good missile shot at him before he forces you inside Rmin.

Gun Shot Procedures

Flying good offensive BFM against a bandit will put him right in your gun sights. You'll get him there by understanding the dynamics of getting into position, closing and firing.

Flying into Gun Parameters

It is time to discuss how and when we turn to stay behind the bandit. You are inside 1.5 nm on a hard turning bandit, and you need turning room to get around on his six. The first step is to observe the bandit's turn. If you are outside the bandit's turn circle, get ready for a head-on BFM fight. If you are near or inside the bandit's turn circle, you have a positional advantage that you can keep. Shoot, if a shot presents itself, but don't get mesmerized watching your own missile and forget to BFM. Next, drive to where the bandit started his turn. If the bandit drops flares or chaff, he will mark the point in the sky where he started his turn. Drive to this position (called the entry window). Figure 2-10 shows the entry window. The entry window is located inside the bandit's turn circle. You can start your high G turn into the bandit once you arrive inside this window.

In Figure 2-10, the F-16 drove in a lag pursuit course to a position inside the bandit's turn circle. By driving to this position, the F-16 gained horizontal turning room that the bandit can't use or take away. You know you are at the entry window and must start your turn when the bandit is approximately 30° off your nose.

When you get into this relationship with the bandit, start your turn. Remember corner velocity. If you arrive at the window too fast or too slow, you will get stuck in lag pursuit because you will not have sufficient turn rate to get your nose out in front of the bandit.

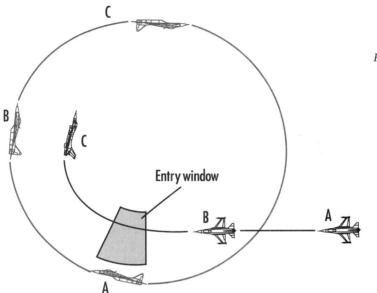

Figure 2-10

The next step is to pull 7 to 8 Gs into the bandit. As you come around the corner, keep your nose in lag. If you see the nose of your jet approaching pure pursuit, ease up on the G. Hold this lag pursuit course until you get within 3,000 feet of the bandit. At this range, go to lead pursuit and get ready for a gun shot.

When you arrive inside 3,000 feet on the bandit with your nose in pure or lead pursuit, your throttle controls your overtake. *Note this.* In close to the bandit, with your angle-off less than 45° and your nose in pure or lead pursuit, the position of your throttle controls your closure. When you get saddled up for a gun shot, you must match airspeed with the target. In most cases, this will require constant movement of the throttle. In addition to banging the throttle off both stops, you may have to maneuver out of plane to control your airspeed. If a throttle reduction and the speed brakes don't slow you down enough, roll the jet to orient your lift vector out of the bandit's plane-of-motion and pull. Hold this lag pursuit pull for about two seconds; then ease off the G and watch the bandit. When he starts to move forward on your canopy, it is time to pull back into him. Pull your lift vector out in front of the bandit as you pull down.

Taking a Gun Shot

You are inside 3,000 feet on the bandit with your nose in lead. How do you take a gun shot? The gun in most fighters is actually a cannon. The F-16, for example, has an M61 20mm cannon which is common to almost every U.S. fighter. The M61 shoots high explosive incendiary (HEI) rounds at the rate of 100 per second. At the proper range, the gun is like a giant buzz saw. In order to carve up the enemy, however, you must understand the fundamentals of taking a gun shot. To hit a target with the gun, you must meet the following conditions:

▸ You must be in range. This range varies, depending on aspect, but it is usually about 2,500 feet at low aspect angles and about 4,000 feet at high aspect.

▸ You must have your nose in lead pursuit. The bullets fired by the gun are unguided projectiles that take time to get to the target. For most gun shots, the bullet time-of-flight (TOF) is .5 to 1.5 seconds. If you point directly at the target and fire, the bullets will pass behind the target. If the bullet moved at the speed of light, you could point right at a turning target and score a hit. Since the bullet is considerably slower, you must pull lead. This lead may not be very pronounced, however, at close range.

▸ You must be in the bandit's plane of motion. When an aircraft turns, it carves a circle in the sky that creates a plane. In order for you to hit the target with the gun, you must be turning in the same plane as your target. For example, if the target is flying a loop and creating a vertically oriented plane of motion, you have to be flying a loop in the same plane as the target.

Using the Gun Sight

The new gun sight for the F-16 and F-15 is called EEGS. EEGS (pronounced as it is spelled) stands for Enhanced Envelope Gun Sight. The EEGS funnel allows the pilot to match the wingspan of the target with the width of the funnel to determine the proper firing range. The other important gun aiming cue in the HUD is the gun cross. The gun cross represents the departure line of the bullets. You can consider the gun cross as the gun barrel. Bullets pass straight out the gun cross.

The Falcon 3.0 simulation features the most prominent aiming cue of EEGS, the EEGS funnel.

Figure 2-11 shows an F-16 HUD with the EEGS funnel and the gun cross.

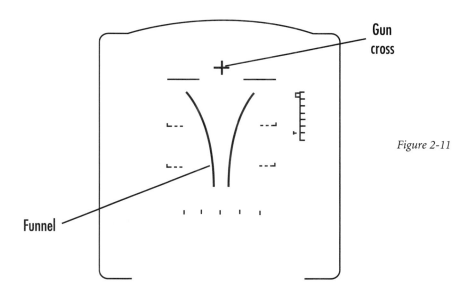

Gun cross

Funnel

Figure 2-11

So, how do you use the funnel? The gun in the F-16 is boresighted to 6 mils. This means that the gun is adjusted to fire a burst that will put 80% of the rounds inside a 6-foot diameter circle at 1,000 feet. This is a tight pattern. You can have either a highly concentrated burst that completely misses the target or a very lethal burst that vaporizes the target. It just depends on the quality of your gun sight (and your ability to aim it.) Air-to-air situations are always dynamic, and targets under attack will normally jink violently to stay alive. Since the sight (and your reactions) are not instantaneous, it is likely you may achieve a highly accurate miss; that is, a tight burst that finds only empty air. The sight was lined up and stable, but you missed. How could this happen? The sight was lying because the target was jinking faster than the sight could react. The way to overcome this problem is to strive for an inaccurate hit. You do this by using the EEGS funnel to fire a burst while moving the target through the area of uncertainty. The EEGS funnel gives you a perfect solution when the wingtips of the target match the width of the funnel. If the target is jinking, however, this "perfect solution" may be in error.

Here is how to use the gun cross/funnel combination to kill the bandit:

pitot boom – a sensor probe on the nose of the F-16

▶ Place the gun cross out in front of the target. Picture the target with a long pitot boom sticking out the nose. The gun cross should be placed on this extended pitot boom. If the target changes his plane-of-motion, then fly to place the gun cross on the new position of this imaginary pole sticking out of the nose of the target.

▶ Next, overlead the target by making the wingspan of the target extend past the funnel. This will place your bullet stream in front of the target's nose.

▶ Fire the gun while easing up on the G. This will move the target from the bottom of the funnel to the top. Cease fire when the target's wings are inside the funnel.

▶ Make a slight jink out of the bandit's plane-of-motion so, when he blows up, you don't suck a body part down your intake.

This technique uses the gun cross and the EEGS funnel to place the bullet stream in front of the bandit. When you ease up on the G, the target should fly through your bullets. Figure 2-12 shows how to make this shot.

Figure 2-12

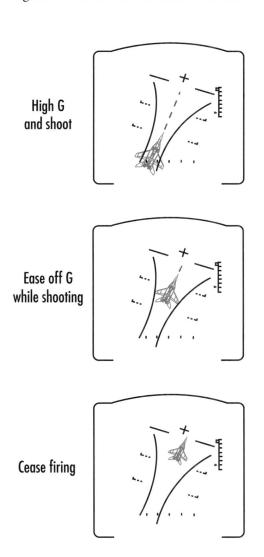

High G and shoot

Ease off G while shooting

Cease firing

Fighter Pilot Training Sorties: Offensive BFM

Here are a few fighter pilot rules of thumb for setting up an offensive BFM training sortie.

▶ There should always be one guy who is getting the training and one guy who is the training aid.

▶ It is easy to set up offensive engagements by first starting line abreast and then executing an in-place turn as shown in the diagram below.

Figure 2-13

After getting in lead-trail formation, the guy out in front should start an easy 30° bank turn and the trailer should use lead to close the range if necessary or go lag to increase the range. Both pilots should be at the proper airspeed. For setups at a mile or greater, this airspeed is 400 to 500 knots. For setups at 3,000 feet, the airspeed of both pilots should be no more than 300 knots. Any airspeed faster than 300 knots at ranges of 3,000 feet or less will cause line-of-sight rates that the offensive fighter cannot handle.

▶ For sake of discussion, we'll call the trailing pilot "Falcon 1-2" and the guy out in front "Falcon 1-1." The fight should start with the trailer saying, "Falcon One-Two is established at 1 mile and ready." The guy out front should say, "Falcon One-One is ready—fight's on."

With the "Fight's on" call, Falcon 1-1 should crank into a defensive turn, forcing Falcon 1-2 to BFM. When flying offensive setups, both guys should fight full speed. If the offensive fighter cannot get into guns position and achieve a kill, the fight should be set up again, with the defender pulling a 5 G level turn. Continue this setup until the offensive guy gets in for a gun shot and then go back to a more dynamic engagement.

Conclusion

Offensive BFM is not as straightforward as it appears at first glance. This chapter contains a lot of talk about turns, turn circles and turning room. On the offensive, you must constantly be aware of your position in relation to the bandit's turn circle. You must also control your airspeed because it is the key to turn performance. A fighter at corner velocity has the best overall turn rate/radius performance—slower or faster speeds degrade turn performance. It sounds simple, but you can spend far too much of your life suffering under tremendous G and not turning the jet because you let the airspeed run away. The message here is this: control your airspeed or you will lose the fight!

Finally, you must also remember to factor in Gs. As you pull Gs, you must place your nose on the proper pursuit course to the target. Remember, on the attack, lag the bandit until you are inside 3,000 feet. At 3,000 feet, go lead for the gun shot but watch your overtake.

The academic lecture on the videotape will polish up your knowledge of offensive BFM. After viewing the offensive BFM section of the tape, you can come back to this book and take the offensive BFM quiz located in "BFM Lesson Plans."

Chapter 3

DEFENSIVE BFM

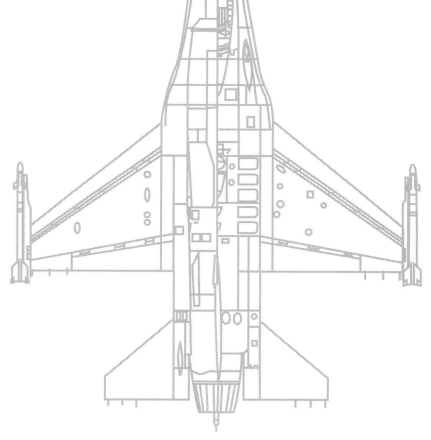

Defensive BFM

I learned the most about fighting defensive BFM while flying as an IP in the F-16A at MacDill AFB. MacDill, as I mentioned earlier, was an F-16 training base. When flying student rides, we seldom fought at full speed, but when we flew sorties against the other IPs, we gave it everything we had. Competition was intense among the instructors, which led to some very rapid learning during BFM rides.

During one particular engagement, I learned the value of keeping your lift vector right on the bandit when performing a defensive turn. This engagement occurred during an instrument check ride. On an instrument check at MacDill, we normally flew down to Southwest Regional Airport near Ft. Myers and did an ILS and an SFO approach. We then entered an over-water range and did some BFM. After finishing our BFM, we went back to MacDill for a TACAN approach and an overhead pattern. A check pilot chased us through all of those maneuvers and graded our performance.

ILS – instrument landing system

SFO – simulated flameout

The guy giving me this particular check ride was named Smitty. Smitty was the Wing Top Gun in bombing and an all-around good flyer. After finishing our work at Southwest Regional, we entered the over-water area and got set up for a perch BFM engagement with me out in front. Smitty found his way back about 7,000 feet, and when we both had about 450 knots, I called "Fight's on." Then I started an 8 G defensive turn to the left with my lift vector right on Smitty's noggin.

Before I go any further, it might be beneficial to explain some of the physical demands that you encounter in the jet when making a defensive turn. I normally describe BFM fights and immediately get engrossed in describing the detailed geometry of the fight, skipping the physical aspects of air combat altogether. Since the chapter you're about to read is on defensive BFM, it might be useful to briefly describe the physical side of the defensive fight. Defensive BFM is one of the most violent physical activities you can undergo (without dying). You must pull high Gs while keeping sight of an enemy at 6 o'clock. Throughout high G maneuvering, you must fight the Gs in order to keep the blood flow to your cranium. You accomplish this by using an L-1 maneuver: a series of 2- to 3-second grunts against a closed windpipe. This maneuver raises your blood pressure, which keeps the sky blue (rather than black) and your brain working. The L-1 manueuver is slightly different from the older M-1 manuever, in which the windpipe is open during the grunts.

The most difficult task to perform under high G is to check 6 o'clock. In an F-16, it's much harder to check 6 when turning to the right because the F-16 stick is on the right side of the cockpit. Since you must keep your right hand on the side stick controller during a turn, you have to twist your body to the right and look over your right shoulder. You actually accomplish this by pulling yourself around with your free left hand. (The throttle is in afterburner and usually stays there so your left hand is free.) The F-16 has a "towel rack" located on both sides of the cockpit. These towel racks are used to help you move around the cockpit when the elephant is sitting on your shoulders. In a right-hand defensive turn, for example, you grab the towel rack on the right side of the cockpit with your left hand, pull yourself to the right, and look over your right shoulder. It's easier to turn to the left to check 6. With your right hand again on the side stick controller, you simply push off the left towel rack, lean to the right, and look over your left shoulder. In the fight with Smitty, I made a left-hand turn. In a left turn, it is relatively easy (as easy as it could be with a 160-pound head) to keep a tally.

Now, back to the fight. I made my turn to the left, and after about 50°, I noticed that Smitty was maneuvering slightly out of plane above me. Great. I rotated my lift vector to keep right on him. He countered by going even higher in the vertical.

Taking a 30,000-pound jet that does not like slow air-speeds in the vertical can be a very unforgiving maneuver. The F-16 flies slow very well as long as you're careful not to assault the flight control computer limiters. The limiters keep you from putting the aircraft out of control. They work best, however, when the jet is fast and the nose is level or below the horizon. In fact, an F-16 adage is "When you are slow and nose high, don't assault the limiters." As you get nose high and slow, a pilot with "Armour Star" hands can fly the jet past the limiters and end up a passenger in a large mass of metal with the flight characteristics of a riding mower. This doesn't mean that you can't get slow and nose high in the F-16. It just means that when you do, you better do it right.

When Smitty drove his jet to a position at my high 6 o'clock, I had to make a decision. Should I continue a safe level turn or keep my lift vector on him and challenge him in the vertical? In truth, there was no choice. If I had stayed level, he would definitely have shot me.

The fight had now gone about 90°, and I had 320 knots of airspeed as I pulled straight up with my lift vector right on Smitty. He was now in the hurt locker because he had 100 knots more airspeed on his jet than I did. This gave him a good turn rate (although not much better than mine) but a very large turn radius. Fighter pilots have a saying that "Radius overshoots," and this is what happened to Smitty. As we both went in the vertical, my smaller turn radius fit inside his bigger turn radius, and he simply flew out in front of me. The only problem I had at this point was controlling the nose of the jet at 130 knots, but luckily for me, Smitty panicked when he saw that I was behind him. He rolled off and went nose low for airspeed. This gave me the chance to pull back down and regain some smash myself. It took about 15 seconds for me to go from a defensive perch setup to a gun kill.

Smitty's primary mistake was getting turning room in the vertical. Turning room, as you know, is used to solve angle-off and aspect problems. It's usually best to get your turning room in the horizontal against a high performance fighter. When Smitty went into the vertical, he gained turning room that both pilots could use. Since we had roughly equal turn rates, and since I had a tighter turn radius, I could use the turning room better than he could and gained the advantage.

The point of this story is that even against a good pilot, you can survive if you force him to make a mistake. In order to do this, however, you must know what to do and then execute it flawlessly.

Introduction to Defensive BFM

The stakes are high when you find yourself on the defensive. Defensive BFM is characterized by difficult, high-G combat, flown while you look out the back of the jet. Since most fighter pilots don't do their best creative thinking twisted around in the cockpit under high Gs, it is best to have a game plan in mind before finding a bandit at your 6 o'clock. We mentioned in Chapter 2 that offensive BFM is not a set of specific moves but rather a series of fluid maneuvers. The same is true when you start with a bandit behind you. There are no magic moves that will move a bandit from your 6 o'clock to your 12 o'clock. In fact, if you fly perfect defensive BFM and the bandit flies perfect offensive BFM, you will get shot down. This statement speaks volumes about defensive BFM.

Defensive BFM is very simple: create BFM problems for the bandit, and when he BFMs, try to counter his BFM to buy time and survive a little longer. By forcing the bandit to BFM, you may force him to make a BFM error that you can capitalize on. If he doesn't make a mistake, he will drive into gun parameters. When this happens, you must be ready to defeat the gun shot.

Detecting the Attack

Before you can defend against an attack, you must detect that you are under attack. Most air-to-air kills are against targets that have no idea that they are about to be stuck. There are three primary methods used to detect an attack:

Radar

Your air-to-air radar is the best way to detect an attack because it can look out past 40 nm. All airborne intercept (AI) radars are limited in azimuth and elevation coverage, so radar will not always warn you that bandits are in your area.

Threat Warning System (TWS)

Your threat warning system can detect if any radars are looking at your jet. Again, TWS threat reactions will be covered during the discussion of the engaged two-ship element in the next book.

Visual

No matter how else you detect an attacking bandit, eventually you will have to get a tally to fight him effectively. This chapter will discuss what to do when you see an attacking bandit.

Defending Against a Missile

Whether you see an attacking bandit or not, you must adhere to a fundamental rule of air combat: "Fight the most immediate threat." You will face a lot of confusing situations as a fighter pilot. To increase your chances of survival, fight the threat that is in the best position to kill you. For example, take a MiG-29 at 6 o'clock that has fired an AA-11 Archer IR missile at you. When that missile leaves the rail and starts guiding on you, the MiG is no longer the biggest threat to your jet. The missile becomes the primary threat, so you must fight the missile.

Here's another fighter pilot axiom to keep in mind: "Fight missiles with aspect." When a missile is fired at your jet in the aft quadrant, the best way to defeat it is with a maximum rate turn to put the missile on the beam (along your 3/9 line). You will give a missile the most guidance problems if you put the missile at your 3 or 9 o'clock position. In this position, you will be at 90° of aspect with respect to the missile, and it will have the worst possible line-of-sight rate problem to solve. Missiles fly lead pursuit courses to the target in order to achieve maximum range. If you hold the missile somewhere on your 3/9 line, you will make the missile pull the maximum amount of lead. You will also be moving across the missile field-of-view at the fastest rate. Figure 3-1 shows this position.

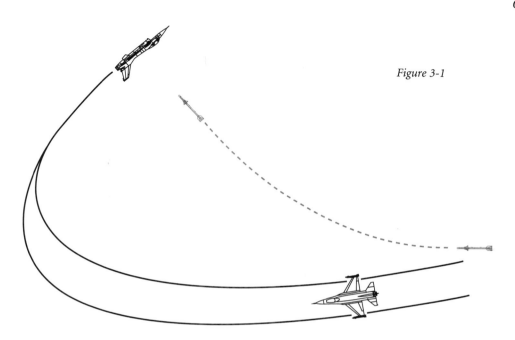

Figure 3-1

In Chapter 2, we discussed max G turns at corner velocity. It is critical that you generate your best turn rate to drive the missile to the beam quickly. Don't think in terms of trying to force the missile to overshoot with a tight turn radius. Missiles are designed to explode as they overshoot you. If they fly past you inside the lethal radius of the warhead, you will be turned into a cloud of body parts. Also, while making a defensive turn to put the missile on the beam, always remember to dispense chaff and flares.

Creating BFM Problems for the Bandit

A bandit shows up at your 6 o'clock. What do you do?

If he fires a missile, fight the missile! But before a missile is fired, you must turn and create BFM problems for the bandit. The defensive turn should be the quickest, tightest turn you can make. There are obvious BFM reasons for doing a high-G turn, but there are psychological reasons as well. An 8 G turn into the bandit will make a clear statement of your intent to remain alive and fight this guy with everything you've got. An 8 G turn says to the bandit, "It is me against you for all the wine and women in world." A 4 to 5 G turn says that you are Little Bo Peep and have somehow managed to take off in a fighter. You will invite slaughter (and deserve it) with a weak turn.

Figure 3-2

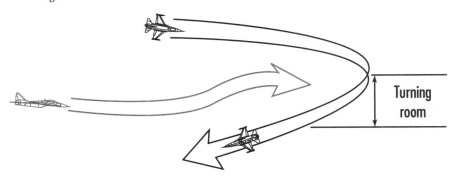

We've already mentioned that in order to get the quickest, tightest turn, you must be at corner velocity. As you start a defensive turn into the bandit, you should place your lift vector directly on him. This will give the bandit the most angle-off and aspect problems to solve. You will also deny him turning room by keeping your lift vector directly on his jet. It is easy to see why turning with your lift vector off of the bandit will give him turning room. In Figure 3-2, you can see a defending F-16 placing his lift vector below the horizon while doing a defensive turn. The attacking MiG-29 stays level and gains turning room above the defender by just driving in level.

Bandit Outside Your Turn Circle

So you have rolled your jet to place your lift vector right on the bandit and executed your best high-G turn at corner velocity. What next?

Now you must determine if your defensive turn is working. If the bandit is being forced forward from 6 o'clock toward your 3 or 9 o'clock position, then the turn is working. A bandit that starts outside your turn circle will be forced in front of your 3/9 line if you perform the defensive turn correctly. Figure 3-3 shows a MiG-29 attacking an F-16. The F-16 pilot turns with his lift vector on the bandit at corner velocity and forces the bandit in front of his 3/9 line.

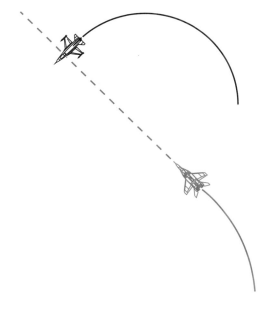

Figure 3-3

Your turn is working if you push a bandit forward towards your nose. Keep in mind that he can still shoot you! If the bandit has his nose in lead as you drive him forward with your defensive turn, be ready to defend against a gun shot. Remember, in order for him to take a gun shot, he needs to meet three conditions: he must be in range, he must be in plane, and he must have his nose in lead pursuit. If the bandit's nose is in lead pursuit, watch out! Even though he will overshoot, the bandit will probably attempt a gun shot at the pass. To defend against this type of gun shot, all you have to do is break suddenly out of plane. Because of the high line-of-sight rates involved, the bandit will not be able to correct in time and will overshoot. A bandit that starts outside your turn circle and drives in with his nose in lead for a gun shot will overshoot. Overshoots are discussed in more detail below.

Bandit Inside Your Turn Circle

What if the bandit starts at 1 nm? Your reaction should be the same. Put your best defensive turn on the bandit and see what he does. When a bandit starts close to your turn circle, he is a serious threat, and your best defensive turn may not force him forward. The bandit has one good option if he is committed to staying around and killing you: he has to fly lag pursuit to get to your turn circle entry window. When a bandit starts inside your turn circle and drives to lag, you are in for a long day. The best course of action is to continue your high-G turn and try to stick his nose in lag. There are some schools of thought that say you should unload the jet (release the G) and extend for energy. The problem with an extension is that it is very hard to judge how long to keep the jet unloaded and driving straight. When you unload and accelerate, the bandit will move quickly to deep 6 o'clock, and you will probably attract an AA-11 shot. The best course of action against a lagging bandit is to continue turning and see if the bandit has a sufficient turn rate to get his nose around on you. If he does, get ready for gun defense. Figure 3-4 shows a MiG-29 flying a good lag entry on an F-16.

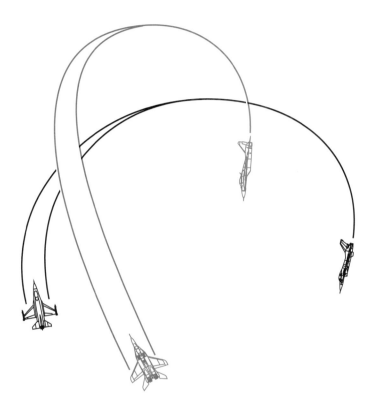

Figure 3-4

The bandit may not fly perfect BFM. What if he climbs above you?

If the bandit pulls into the vertical for turning room, keep the hard turn coming with your lift vector directly on the him. As you pull up into the bandit, watch him. If he immediately pulls down to a lag position as you pull up into him, he knows what he is doing and will quickly close the range for a gun shot. If he keeps his nose high, you will end up in a neutral position on the bandit because you are slower and have a smaller turn radius. Since you have just started your turn, you should still have enough energy and turn rate ability to get around the corner and pass the bandit at high angles. Figure 3-5 shows this type of fight.

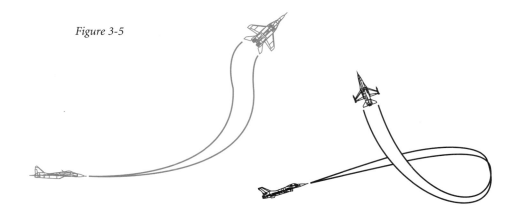

Figure 3-5

In this type of fight, you will end up in a scissors. Scissors occur when two fighters are in a line-abreast, neutral position. They both pull for each other's 6 o'clock position and, as they pass, they roll back into each other and pull. The scissors is usually won by the fighter that can slow his forward velocity, in relation to the bandit, the quickest. Figure 3-6 shows a scissors.

Lead pursuit is another attack pursuit course that the bandit may take. If a bandit starts at 1 nm back and flies a lead pursuit course, he will probably overshoot. Remember the 2 nm setup already discussed? The same result will occur at 1 nm. In order to force the bandit to overshoot, however, you must be executing your best turn. The bandit will not overshoot if you are 50 or more knots slower or faster than corner velocity, or if you are not pulling enough G.

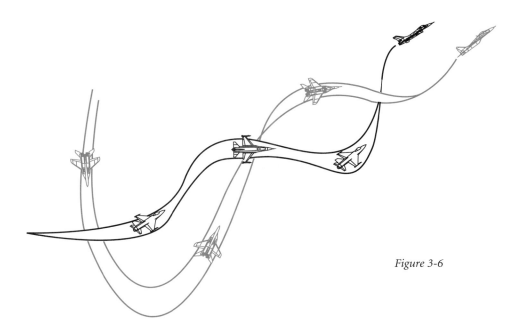

Figure 3-6

The last option the bandit has is a pure pursuit attack. If you see a bandit pointing at you and a missile is not coming off of his jet, you are in for a treat. A guy that points at you for more than a few seconds is clueless. This type of maneuvering is called HUD BFM. HUD BFM almost always results in a gross overshoot and a lead change—in other words, the bandit will end up in front.

Overshoots

There are two type of overshoots: the flight path overshoot and the 3/9 line overshoot. A 3/9 line overshoot is always tactically significant, while a flight path overshoot may not be. Figure 3-7 shows a 3/9 line overshoot along with two flight path overshoots. Aircraft A in Figure 3-7 slightly overshoots the F-16's flight path. This is not tactically significant. Aircraft B, on the other hand, overshoots the F-16's flight path far enough that he may end up line-abreast or out in front if the F-16 reverses his turn. Aircraft C is obviously in big trouble because he has blundered past the F-16's 3/9 line. All overshoots are not created equal.

Figure 3-7

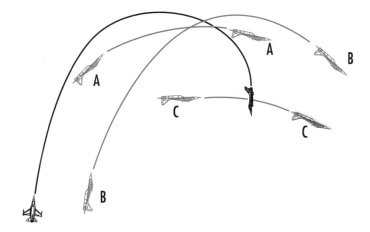

When you predict that a bandit may overshoot, note the range, angle-off, and the line-of-sight rate of the bandit. His position, in relation to you, will dictate how you will reverse. As a rule of thumb, the greater the range when he overshoots and the slower the line-of-sight rate, the less chance you have of forcing him out in front of your 3/9 line with a reversal.

When a bandit overshoots, there are basically two ways to reverse your turn to take advantage of it. If you see the bandit is going to overshoot with a high line-of-sight rate, you should perform an unloaded reversal. To do an unloaded reversal, simply release the G, roll the aircraft to position your lift vector directly on the bandit, and then pull maximum G directly at him. You should only use this reversal method when you are sure that the bandit will overshoot. This type of reversal does not "force" the bandit out in front of you; it just gets your nose on the bandit quickly when he does overshoot.

The other type of reversal should be used with caution. It is called a loaded reversal. To execute a loaded reversal, keep the Gs on the jet as you roll and pull toward the bandit. This type of reversal is used to "force" a bandit that is about to overshoot *into* an overshoot. Figure 3-8 shows this type of situation.

Figure 3-8

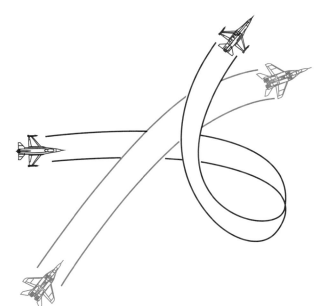

The problem with a loaded reversal is that, if you execute it and the bandit doesn't overshoot, you will have a bad guy in your chili at close range, and you won't have the airspeed to maneuver. A loaded reversal is used to stop your aircraft in the sky, and if doesn't work, you're in trouble. For this reason, let's go over a few overshoot rules of thumb.

▸ When in doubt about a bandit's overshoot, don't reverse your turn.

▸ It is best to reverse when a bandit is overshooting your flight path inside 2,000 feet with a high line-of-sight rate.

▸ Outside 3,000 feet, it is best not to reverse your turn. The bandit has too much room to correct his overshoot and maintain a 3/9 advantage on you.

Guns Defense

You have flown perfect defensive BFM, but the bandit has flown perfect offensive BFM and is closing for a gun shot. What should you do?

Snapshots and Tracking Shots

There are basically two types of gun shots: the high line-of-sight snapshot and the stabilized tracking gun shot. This chapter has already briefly explained how to defend against a snapshot. When a bandit is closing with a high line-of-sight rate on your jet with his nose in lead, think "snapshot." A snapshot is usually not the result of perfectly flown BFM, but it can still kill you. To defend against a snapshot, you should break out of plane. The only tough part is judging when to make your move. It is better to make it too soon rather than too late. If you go early, the bandit can correct, but when he does, you can jink out of plane again. If you jink late, you may end up having a valuable appendage carved off by the bandit's gun.

How about tracking gun shots? These are harder to defend against because the bandit is not passing his gun through you quickly, as he does in a snapshot. In a tracking gun shot, the bandit is in a stable position behind you and will take multiple shots. For this reason, you will have to make multiple out-of-plane jinks to keep from getting shot. The key to guns defense is to make sudden jinks at least 70° out of plane with the attacker. Keep a tally on the bandit, and before he gets established in this new plane of motion, jink again. This type of defense is a random guns jink.

The Snake

A popular guns jink, currently in vogue in the F-16 community, is the "snake." Here's how you do it: when you see the bandit pulling his nose into lead, you unload rapidly, roll 180°, and reverse your direction of turn. Hold this course and make the bandit pull his nose back into lead. If the bandit reduces power to stay behind you, he may end up getting stuck in lag. If his nose is stuck in lag, keep turning with your lift vector above the horizon.

If the bandit has the energy to get his nose back into lead, unload again and roll 180° to reverse your turn again. This time, reduce power to bait him into an overshoot. As the bandit repositions to lead pursuit, unload and roll 180° again and reduce power further. If you have lived this long, you should be jamming the bandit and forcing an overshoot. Anytime you see that the bandit is going to overshoot, get back into full burner, set your wings level with the horizon and pull max G. This will help him fly out in front of your 3/9 line.

This maneuver is not a magic move. If the bandit is highly skilled, he will probably gun you—snake or no snake. It is worth a try, however, because against a plumber, it will work almost every time. If you're lucky, you might get a chance to see *his* best guns defense.

Fighter Pilot Training Sorties: Defensive BFM

When a fighter pilot practices defensive BFM, it is important that the offensive fighter fight at reduced power or make some pronounced BFM errors. If both guys have similar abilities and fight full speed (no restrictions on the use of the throttle), and if the offensive fighter starts at 1 nm, the defensive fighter will get killed and will not get a chance to do anything but a guns jink. Here are some defensive BFM scenarios.

In Scenarios 1–4, both fighters should fly at corner velocity.

Scenario #1

The offensive fighter starts at 2 nm. Both fighters fight at full speed, but no missile shots are allowed until either fighter completes 180° of turn.

Scenario #2

The offensive fighter starts at 1 nm and pulls immediately into the vertical. After getting 40° nose-high, the offensive fighter is free to maneuver as necessary.

Scenario #3

The offensive fighter starts at 1 nm and flies a lead pursuit course all the way in for a gun shot. Both fighters fight at full speed, except that the offensive fighter must maintain a lead pursuit course until the overshoot.

Scenario #4

The offensive fighter starts at 1 nm and fights his best BFM, but at reduced power.

Scenario #5

The offensive fighter starts at 3,000 feet and 300 knots. The defensive fighter is at corner velocity. The offensive fighter fights at full speed but does not take a shot until the defensive fighter makes his first break out of plane.

Use the same "Fight's on" call described in Chapter 2 to start each fight.

Conclusion

Defensive BFM is straightforward. Pull hard with your lift vector right on the bandit and watch what he does. If he makes a mistake, capitalize on it. If he drives to a lag entry window, keep fighting, but you will probably end up doing a guns defense. It is critical that you maintain the will to survive when fighting defensively. Never give up. Push the aircraft to maximum performance at all times.

The "Defensive BFM" academic lecture on the videotape will help reinforce the material in this chapter. After watching the tape, you can take the quiz in "BFM Lesson Plans."

Chapter 4

HEAD-ON BFM

Head-on BFM

It was just another BFM ride with a new lieutenant in the squadron. This lieutenant, who will remain nameless, was a pretty solid flyer according to his training gradebook. On this mission, we were going to fly one offensive, one defensive, and one head-on BFM setup. The lieutenant did reasonably well on the offensive and defensive setups—nothing to write home about, but not too bad. The last engagement was the head-on fight, and this is where the real action started.

Before describing this engagement, I better take a minute to relate how the flight briefing went. On a head-on setup with a new guy, I usually brief that I will fight in military power. In other words, I will not use the afterburner. This is just a standard way I do this type of sortie.

Well, I was in the process of briefing the ride this way when this lieutenant interrupts my briefing and offers his opinion on the subject. Now we usually don't have a lot of "open forum" briefings. If the flight lead asks the flight for their opinion, they provide it. If he doesn't ask, then everybody keeps his mouth shut and executes the mission as briefed. Period. So, here I am briefing the mission to a brand-new guy just back from training and he interrupts me with a creative thought. Creative thoughts are good, and I have nothing against them. Orville and Wilbur had a few good ones, but there haven't been many since then, and I severely doubted that this kid had one now. It turned out that I was right. It seems that he didn't think that it was such a good idea that I fight him in military power because he would kill me too easily and not get a chance to practice any real BFM on that engagement. I successfully fought the impulse to burst out laughing and politely told him that we would do it anyway. He could just get some more gun tracking practice with me as a target.

There are several ways you can get into a head-on BFM engagement. One way is to get 25 miles apart and then do an intercept to an engagement. The most fuel-efficient way of getting into a head-on fight is to do a butterfly entry. On a butterfly, the two fighters start line abreast and then turn 45° away from each other. When they get about four miles apart, they turn back into a head-on pass. They can make a "Fight's on" call as they start to turn back into each other, or they can call "Fight's on" as they pass head-on.

I briefed a butterfly setup that started as we passed. At this point in my fighter pilot career, I've flown hundreds of head-on engagements and normally don't get too excited about it. Because of the lieutenant's comments in the briefing, however, I was wired for this one. At the pass, I immediately executed a move in the pure vertical. I don't normally like to go up first, but when I am limited to fighting in military power, a move in the vertical at the pass can sometimes work. As I went up at 7 Gs, I leaned my head straight back and picked up a tally on the opponent below me. When I reached the pure vertical, I rotated my lift vector right on him and pulled over the top toward his jet. He had executed a nose-low, high-G slice and was around the corner and pulling up into me as I pulled down into him. His nose was on me first, and he had about a 40° advantage as we approached, with me nose-low and him nose-high. We passed "highway style," and it appeared that the fight would go two-circle in right-hand turns.

highway style – left to left

Appearances, though, can be deceiving. As we passed, I quickly rolled 180° and reversed my turn to the left changing the engagement to a one-circle fight. The lieutenant had done everything right up to this point. He had executed a good nose-low slice and had gained angles on a limited-thrust aircraft. He had maintained his energy as he entered what he thought was a two-circle fight and was attempting to lead turn at the pass. He expected the fight to stay two-circle (since most fights do), and he knew he had more airspeed and a better sustained turn rate with the use of the after-burner. So he passed my jet and kept turning right.

As he looked out of the right side of the cockpit, he was shocked to see my jet across the circle in a left-hand turn pulling toward him. I could tell he was surprised because he did what most inexperienced guys do in this situation. He just kept pulling toward me in a horizontal turn. This turn lasted a few seconds, long enough for him to start to fly out in front of me. His superior thrust and greater airspeed gave him a bigger turn radius, and I simply fit my smaller radius inside his, in this one-circle fight. I was in military power, so I was at least 100 knots slower at this point. He still had a big advantage, but he could not convert it into a kill. When you are new in the air combat game, you frequently reach down into your bag of tricks and pull out a hand-ful of lint. That's what happened here. The lieutenant just rode that big GE engine around a horizontal circle that was too big, with a great big question mark suspended over the his canopy. I quickly gained a 3/9 line advantage and got a chance to practice *my* gun tracking. It was over very fast.

What happened here? The main problem for my opponent was that he had not seen a move like this before, so he wasn't sure what to do. When I took the fight one circle, he should have gone into the vertical. I had very poor energy relative to his jet at this point, and he could have gained turning room above me. He could have then converted this turning room into a 3/9 line advantage. Another thing he did wrong was to get overconfident. The moral here is that there are no predetermined outcomes in air combat. Even when you start with an advantage, you must fly smart to win, starting with the fundamentals of modern fighter head-on BFM, which you will learn in this chapter.

Introduction to Head-on BFM

A head-on BFM fight requires more maneuvering than any other fight we have discussed so far. As you approach an enemy fighter head-on, you have two options: you can separate or you can stay and fight. The biggest decision you must make when passing a bandit head-on is whether you should get anchored in a turning fight. If you enter a fight with a bandit from head-on, you will use up both energy and time. Energy is needed to maneuver, and time can be used against you by yet another bandit who may find your fight and get in on you for a shot. If you take too much time, you may be winning the fight you started with one bandit, but losing a fight with a second bandit you don't see.

There are many good reasons to blow past the bandit and separate. There are also plenty of times when you will have to turn and fight. This chapter will provide the academic background to help you construct a game plan for fighting a bandit from head-on. Before plunging into head-on BFM, you need to understand the concept of the "escape window."

The Escape Window

A fighter pilot enters a fight to shoot down the enemy and survive to fight another day. As you enter a fight, you must be aware of your position in regard to your escape window. The escape window represents your safe path out of the fight. Said another way, the window represents your chances of separating from the fight. The window expands and contracts based on both the geometry of fight and your energy. If you jump a single bandit that doesn't have a tally, your escape window is huge. You can leave the fight at anytime. However, if the bandit picks up a tally and starts a defensive turn, your escape window starts to shrink. As the window shrinks, the probability of getting out of the fight goes down. At some point in a maneuvering fight, your escape window closes completely. Figure 4-1a shows an offensive BFM setup with the attack-

ing fighter inside the bandit's turn circle at low angle-off.
Is the escape window open or closed?

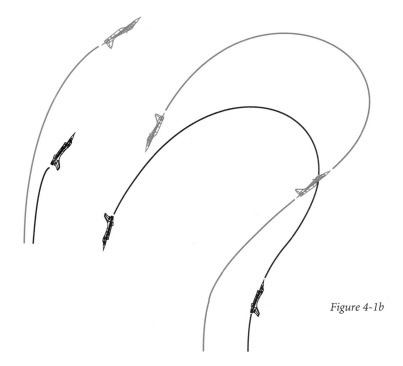

Figure 4-1a

Figure 4-1b

In this engagement, the escape window is closed. Figure
4-1b shows why. At low angle-off, inside the bandit's turn
circle, the attacker cannot get out of the fight. If he tries to
leave the fight, the bandit will just reverse his turn and
stick the attacker with a missile. The escape window for the
bandit is definitely closed. Since neither fighter can get out
of this engagement, somebody is going to the meat locker.
The defensive fighter knows that he can't get out of this
fight. The offensive fighter may not know the window is
closed. Lots of guys try to dive out of a closed escape window, only to get hosed in the attempt.

Figure 4-2a shows another offensive BFM setup. Is the offensive fighter's escape window opened or closed in this engagement?

Figure 4-2a

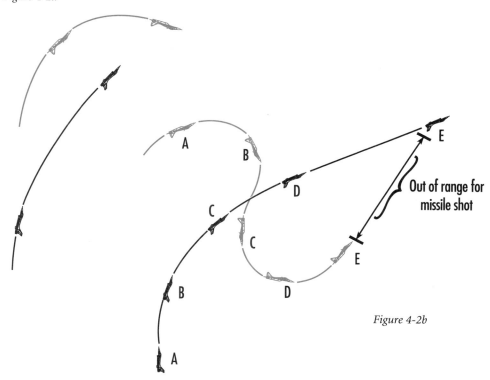

Figure 4-2b

It is open. Figure 4-2b illustrates why. When you are outside the bandit's turn circle, you can get your nose to lead pursuit early enough in the fight to pass the bandit with high angle-off and high speed. You also force the bandit to turn back 180° to put his nose on you after already turning 180° to meet you with high angles. Since the bandit will be slow, your escape window will be open throughout this engagement. What would happen if the attacker drove into lag pursuit and then turned aggressively to put his nose on the bandit? The escape window would close.

In Figure 4-3, two fighters have entered what we call a Lufbery. They are across the circle from each other, pulling to gain an advantage. Can either one of them get out of this fight? No. Again, the first one that tries to leave, dies.

Figure 4-3

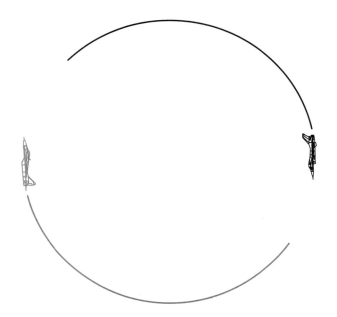

Do not conclude from this discussion that the purpose of air combat is to fly around and keep your escape window open. If you want to be really safe, you should stay on the ground, holding hands with sweet Marie. If you are going to strap on a fighter, you will have to hang it out at some point, in order to kill the enemy. As you enter a fight, however, you should be aware of what your escape window is doing, so you won't get caught trying to dive out a closed escape window.

Stay and Fight? Or Separate?

So what affects your escape window? Assuming everybody in the fight has a tally (an assumption that is seldom correct), the following factors drive the position of your escape window:

▶ Your range from the bandit: the greater the range, the more "open" the escape window.

▶ Your energy relative to the bandit: the greater your energy, the more "open" your escape window.

▶ Your combined angle-off and aspect with the bandit: a head-on pass gives you the best chance for an open escape window.

As you enter a head-on fight, your escape window is usually open. Think carefully before you turn and slam it shut.

Lead Turns

A **lead turn** is an attempt to decrease angle-off prior to passing the bandit's 3/9 line. Lead turning is one of the most important concepts in BFM. Lead turns can be used anywhere, but they are used most often in head-on BFM. Lead turns are the most energy efficient way to BFM. Stated more directly, if one fighter lead turns and the other fighter does not, the lead turning fighter will win. Here's how you execute a lead turn.

As you approach a bandit head-on, watch the line-of-sight rate of the bandit. When you approach an aircraft head-on, it will be relatively stationary on your canopy. As you get closer, the bandit will start to move aft on your canopy. There is a place in space and time, just as you pass the bandit, where the closure will transition from high positive numbers to high negative numbers. What this means is that, as you approach the bandit, the V_c (pronounced "V sub C") is high. Your jets are closing on each other at about 1,000 knots since, head-on, V_c will be the sum of your airspeeds. As you pass the bandit's 3/9 line in this example, the V_c will change rapidly from plus 1,000 knots to negative 1,000 knots. When the V_c starts to change from positive to negative, it is time to start your lead turn.

Unfortunately, there is no lead turn light in the cockpit and watching the V_c in the HUD while simultaneously watching the bandit is very difficult. The best way to judge when to start a lead turn is to watch the bandit's line-of-sight rate across your canopy. When it starts to increase rapidly, start your turn. This spot where the line-of-sight rate of the bandit increases is usually very close to 30° off your nose. Figure 4-4 shows an F-16 lead turning a MiG-29.

Figure 4-4

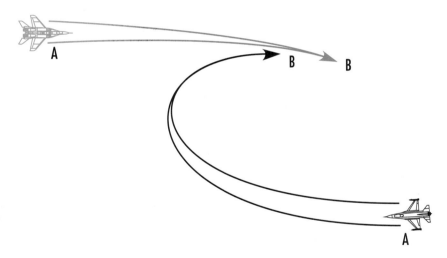

How about the turn itself? Usually lead turns are done at the maximum G possible. When you lead turn, you are closing your escape window and committing yourself to maneuvering combat. Lead turns can be initiated from all aspects and angles-off, but you need to predict the flight path of the bandit and take care not to fly out in front of him while you are doing your lead turn. Figure 4-5 shows a lead turn that is initiated too soon.

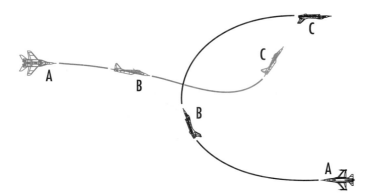

Figure 4-5

There is one particular situation where a lead turn can be used to dominate an adversary. This is the nose-high-to-nose-low pass. Nose-high and nose-low refer to the position of an aircraft's nose in relation to the horizon. When you are nose-high and passing a bandit who is nose-low, it is time to do a big lead turn at max G. You will have the benefit of using the extra radial G caused by gravity, and the bandit will have to fight gravity. If you blunder into this situation or cleverly maneuver the bandit into this situation, you should be able to use a lead turn to gain an immediate 3/9 line advantage. Figure 4-6 shows a nose-high-to-nose-low lead turn.

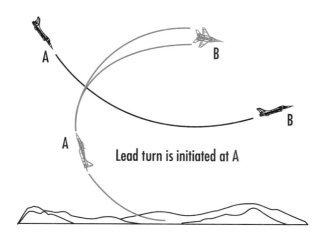

Lead turn is initiated at A

Figure 4-6

You may ask, "If a lead turn is such a potent maneuver, won't the bandit be lead turning my jet?" The answer is "Yes, he will." The best way to negate the effects of a bandit's lead turn is with a lead turn of your own. If you and your clone are both flying F-16s and you each perform a lead turn into the other, the net effect is zero. If you are in an F-16, however, and a bandit is in a MiG-29, and you each perform a lead turn into the other, you will gain a slight advantage, since you have a better-turning jet. The way to counter a lead then is with a lead turn of your own.

Options at the Pass

As you approach a bandit head-on, one of your first thoughts should be "How can I get this over with quick?" Shoot a heat missile if you can, and don't forget the gun. In most head-on passes, you will have to sacrifice BFM to shoot the gun, so it is not advisable to try to line up for a gun shot. If you are committed to separate, however, you should think about a head-on gun shot. Consider that he might also be lining up for a gun shot against you, and even if he isn't, head-on gun shots are dangerous because of the high midair-collision potential. For the sake of our discussion, let's assume you are not going to take a gun shot and you've decided to stay and fight. Here are your options:

pitch back – a climbing high-G turn that ends with the aircraft heading in the opposite direction

split-S – a maneuver that rolls the aircraft 180° to an inverted position, pulls the nose through the horizon and ends up wings-level, heading in the opposite direction

▶ You can turn nose low.

▶ You can turn level.

▶ You can go straight up in the vertical.

You can do a few other things, like pitch back or split-S, but if you see these type of moves on a head-on pass, it normally indicates that the bandit is in the wrong profession. He should be showing a fat lady something in a size 10D pump instead of fighting you in a fighter.

Anyway, before deciding which maneuver to execute from the options we just mentioned, keep in mind this fighter pilot axiom: "Head-on fights are lost and not won." Head-on fights require a lot of maneuvering, so the odds that one of the players will make a mistake is high. The biggest mistake made during head-on BFM is losing sight of the bandit. Since you can't fight what you can't see, this is a sure way to get your knickers ripped. The absolute best BFM move is no good if you lose sight of the bandit halfway through the maneuver. Some other common head-on BFM mistakes are insufficient G, poor airspeed control, bad lift vector control, failure to lead turn, and trying to BFM in an F-14. (Just kidding on that last one—well, not really.)

So, we are committed to a head-on fight. Let's talk about each option.

Nose-Low: The Slice

The quickest way to get your nose around on the bandit is by initiating a lead turn slice into the bandit. To do this maneuver, start an immediate 8 G lead turn into the bandit with your nose about 10° below the horizon when the line-of-sight rate of the bandit starts to increase. By pulling around with your nose low, you will gain the use of gravity which will preserve your airspeed and increase your effective turn rate. (Remember radial G?)

Figure 4-7

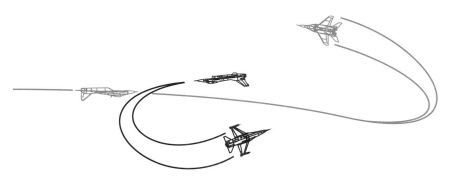

The slice is one of the Viper (F-16) pilot's favorite moves. The reason is simple. The F-16 can out-turn anything in the sky, so a big lead turn executed nose-low will intimidate the bandit. After completing the turn, you will have gained angles on the bandit and still have plenty of energy for the next turn. The disadvantage of the slice is that it is a high-G, nose-low maneuver that places the bandit at deep six and out of sight momentarily. This is not too big a disadvantage if you know where to look for him as you come out of the turn. The bandit should be slightly above the horizon and approaching your 12 o'clock as you complete 180° of turn. Figure 4-7 shows a slice.

The Level Turn

Another good option at the pass is a level turn into the bandit. This option does not get your nose around as fast as the slice, but it has a big advantage over the slice—you can usually maintain a tally throughout the turn. You perform the level turn the same way as you do the slice, except you drag your nose straight across the horizon. Besides slowing down your turn rate, the level turn will slow your airspeed more than the slice does. Don't forget to lead turn when you execute this maneuver.

The Vertical Fight

The last option is a straight pull-up into the vertical. This move is only included for a few special cases. If you are fighting a bandit and the sun is directly overhead, you may want to consider a pull-up into the vertical. Remember, head-on fights are usually lost and not won. If you take the sun on your first move, the bandit may lose sight. You can usually tell when a bandit has lost sight because he does a "Magellan Act." You will see him S-turn and rock his wings trying to pick up tally. His lift vector will probably not be pointing at you as he flails around.

There is another related advantage of a move into the vertical—you will have a lot of aircraft planform to look at, so it is easy to maintain a tally. The big disadvantage of this move is that your initial turn rate is poor as you fight gravity on the pull-up. At the top, of course, you have gravity's help, so your turn rate goes back up. Unfortunately, the bandit will have made some angles on you by then. Another disadvantage of going into the pure vertical is that you present a very hot target, from the heat plume of your jet exhaust, against a very cold sky background. This, coupled with the fact that the bandit has probably gained some angle advantage, might lead you to grief. As a general rule, don't go into the vertical on the first move.

If you must go into the vertical, here is how you do it. As you pass the bandit, start a wings-level pull at 550 knots or as close to 550 as you can get. This is not corner velocity, but it doesn't matter. As you start your 7 G pull, you will bleed off knots like sweat off a pig. Figure 4-8 shows this initial move in the vertical and how much altitude you will gain on the bandit by pulling straight up, rather than turning in the oblique (somewhere in between horizontal and vertical).

Figure 4-8

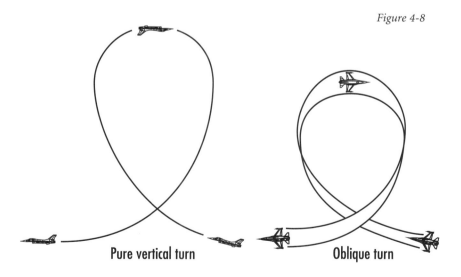

Pure vertical turn   **Oblique turn**

As you get to the pure vertical (straight up), pick up the bandit and pirouette to rotate your lift vector right on him. When your lift vector is on him, pull down. If he sees you, he will pull up into you. At this point, you will be on the receiving end of the nose-high-to-nose-low lead turn. In this situation, counter the lead turn by starting a lead turn of your own. After you counter the lead turn, continue around in a level turn to put your lift vector on the bandit.

The other option is to continue the vertical fight. If you do this, go up again and do not wait until you get 550 knots. When you have 300 knots and are passing the bandit, pull into the vertical. If you delay your pull up, the bandit will gain angles on you. Once you get to the pure vertical, repeat the pirouette and pull. You know you are winning this fight when the bandit no longer pulls his nose up into you. This is a sign that he is out of energy. You now own the turning room above the bandit and can use it to convert on him.

Over-the-Top Airspeed

Here is a story that will you give some insight into how this is done in the F-16.

Students selected to attend the Fighter Weapons School are highly experienced instructor pilots from all over the Tactical Air Force. Before we send a pilot off to be chewed up by the Weapons School meat grinder, we normally give him a few prep rides. I was one of the Weapons and Tactics Officers at MacDill Air Force Base who used to fly with these guys to get them up to speed. The Wing Commander at MacDill did not want to see any of them back early with their tail between their legs, so we put together an extensive BFM course at MacDill to get them ready. BFM is the toughest part of the Weapons School, so this course got the pilots ready to go straight up and straight down in the big leagues.

One day, I fought a guy named Butch. Butch was a good IP with above-average hands, so I figured we would both break a few blood vessels. On the first setup, I was out in front about 6,000 feet. The fight started, and Butch drove right into the entry window and turned the lag corner with the style and grace of a pro. I fought hard but ended up getting shot with the gun after a few violent jinks. Earlier, I had briefed Butch on the dangers of using the vertical during the drive into the turn circle, and he had taken it to heart and killed me quickly.

The next setup started with me out front again at 2 nm. I was not in a good mood due to the results of the previous fight. Even though the student did exactly what I briefed him to do, it is never any fun getting shot. Show me a fighter pilot who doesn't mind getting shot, and I'll show you a guy who should be giving chickens enemas in his veterinary practice instead of riding around on a 30,000-pound blowtorch. Since fighter pilots are bred for combat, most of them feel like I felt after this first engagement—disgusted and irate.

When Butch got back at 2 nm, we called "Fight's on" and I rolled the jet to put my lift vector right on Butch's noggin. This roll was followed by an 8 G break that caused the bright blue Florida sky to fade to black. I kept the pull going, even though my vision was fading, until I knew I was around the corner. I eased up on the G to re-acquire a tally and found Butch quickly moving forward on the canopy. A 2 nm setup is really a head-on fight if the guy out front pulls hard enough. I was definitely pulling hard enough to force Butch in front of the 3/9 line.

As we passed close at high angles, I estimated that Butch had plenty of knots on his jet and I had gotten slow in my pull. This was normal because I had to pull all the way around to meet him at high angles and all he had to do was drive in on me. Because I was down to 250 knots, I released the G and accelerated the jet for a few seconds. When I got back to 400 knots, I put my lift vector back on Butch and started a 7 G pull. While I was extending for knots, Butch had kept pulling at maximum G, and he was back at about 7:30 on me at 1 nm. My turn quickly drove him forward to my 9 o'clock position. The 7 G turn cost me about 200 knots and placed Butch and me in a Lufbery. We were both pulling on the limiter across a 3,000 foot circle with nowhere to go. As I looked at Butch, I could tell that he was about 50 knots slower than me. We went around for 180° and the fight stayed the same, except we both spent another 50 knots in a futile attempt to gain angles. It is precisely in these type of situations that I dust off the old high-low trick maneuver. This maneuver converts the fight from the horizontal to the vertical.

I eased off on the G to gain knots, but kept my wings set to mask the move. As I slowly accelerated, I gave up position and Butch started gaining angles and getting behind me. Before he could get around for a shot, I had reached "over the top airspeed" which, for the F-16, is 250 knots. I suddenly rolled wings-level and started a pull straight up. As I got to the 90° point, I looked back to see what Butch was doing. I wasn't sure if he knew what to do in this situation. When I picked up a tally on Butch, he was still pulling, trying to complete his turn and get his nose uphill on me. Now I was sure that he didn't know how to fight in the vertical. He was a dead man.

After reaching the 90° point, I rolled to put my lift vector on him, and pulled over the top to wings-level, inverted. I did not pull down into him. He still had not unloaded to gain enough energy to follow me up, so now all I had to do was stay above him and fly around to his 6 o'clock. I owned the turning room above him, since he did not have the energy to maneuver in the vertical. Turning room belongs to the guy who can use it most efficiently, and since I was the only one who could use it, I now had the advantage in the fight. I drove above him for a few seconds and then sliced down behind him. His jet continued to wallow around at 120 knots as I gunned him.

What should Butch have done? When a bandit maneuvers vertical and you do not have the energy to follow him up, you are defensive. It is usually no problem because all you have to do is accelerate and then go up with him. If the bandit goes into the oblique, you can stay with him sometimes without accelerating. When a bandit goes straight up, however, he knows what he is doing, and you must get to over-the-top airspeed and follow him up. If a fight is in the vertical and you can get your nose on the bandit, remember to lead turn out the top of the circle and lag out the bottom. This way you won't overshoot down the back side. All Butch needed to do was to unload for airspeed and then follow me up.

Don't get too wrapped around the axle with this explanation of the vertical fight. It's included only because you may have an opportunity in a head-on fight to take advantage of a bandit who has gotten slow. When this happens, you can convert the fight into the vertical, as I did in the fight with Butch, and gain turning room that the bandit can't use. The time to use the vertical fight is after you pass the bandit the third time using one of the first two options. If you can tell he is slow, you may want to take it into the vertical. How do you know if a bandit is slow? He can't rate his nose.

Remember, if you are committed to going vertical, roll wings-level and make your initial pull straight up. Then roll to find the bandit and pull for him. Do not go into the oblique, or you will give the bandit turning room. An old fighter pilot saying from the Vietnam era is "You meet a better class of people in the vertical." This is still true today.

Basic Geometry: One-Circle and Two-Circle Fights

The options that we discussed at the pass can result in either a one-circle or two-circle fight. If both fighters start a lead turn, the fight will go two-circle, as shown in Figure 4-9. This means that two distinct turn circles are created.

Figure 4-9

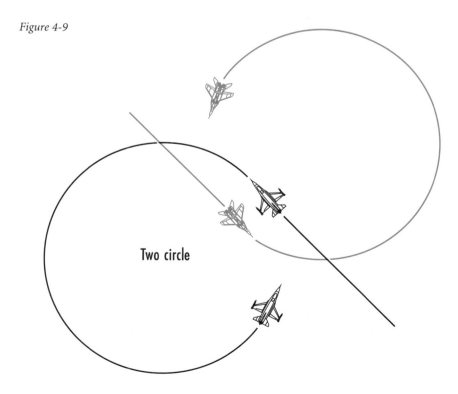

Two circle

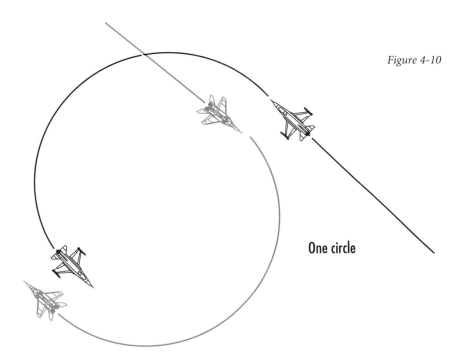

Figure 4-10

One circle

If one of the players turns away, then the fight goes one-circle, as shown in Figure 4-10.

Keep in mind that either you or the bandit can force a one- or two-circle fight. A fighter pilot should understand the characteristics of both of these types of fights. Most head-on passes result in two-circle fights. The reason for this is simple. Usually, fighters lead turn into each other to use the turning room available in an attempt to reduce angle-off. If you are offset from the bandit and turn away, you are not using the turning room available, but worse yet, you are letting him use it. Figure 4-11 shows a case where turning away from the bandit will cause you problems.

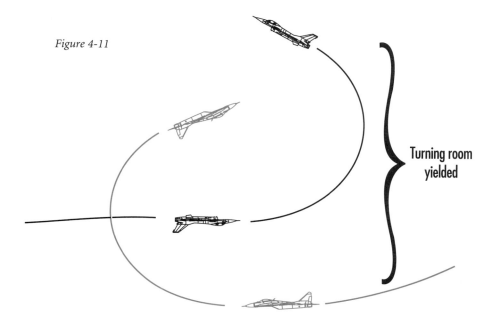

Figure 4-11

Turning room
yielded

Two-circle fights have another advantage for an aircraft with a high turn rate and an all-aspect heat missile. You may be able to get your nose around fast enough to get a shot at the bandit. A one-circle fight is far too tight for a heat missile shot after the pass. In fact, that is the principal reason for taking a fight one-circle. If you are in a fighter without an all-aspect heat missile, you should try to jam the bandit's missile by going one-circle.

A last word about one-circle and two-circle fights. Once you have started your turn, don't reverse it. In other words, if you want to go two-circle but the bandit turns away from you, just keep turning. You will give up far too many angles by taking the time to reverse your turn.

Fighter Pilot Training Sorties: Head-on BFM

These sorties will help you understand the principles of head-on BFM. In these sorties, the opponents will fight a few different types of aircraft. This will help you develop game plans for each enemy aircraft. Here, you will discover that if you are flying a superior turning aircraft, like the F-16, a lead turning fight, either level or nose-low into the bandit, is the most efficient way to turn energy into a weapons shot.

About the Training Sorties

When practicing head-on BFM in similar aircraft (such as two F-16s), it is important that one fighter fly as a training aid for the other. When you are flying two similar aircraft, one fighter will fight at a disadvantage, as outlined in the scenarios below.

In all the scenarios below, the fighter that is practicing his BFM is full up (that is, he has no restrictions on his throttle setting). This fighter should arrive at the head-on pass at whatever airspeed is necessary to execute his head-on BFM game plan. The other fighter's parameters are discussed below, along with the mechanics of the fight. There are two primary ways that fighter pilots practice head-on engagements. The first is that no fighter can maneuver until 3/9 line is passed. The other way to practice head-on engagement is to allow maneuvering as soon as both fighters see each other.

Scenario #1

Head-on pass with a "Fight's on" call as soon as one fighter passes the 3/9 line of the other. One fighter is full up, and the other is restricted to military power.

Scenario #2

Head-on pass with a "Fight's on" call when both fighters have a tally. One fighter is full up, and the other is restricted to military power.

Scenario #3

Head-on pass with a "Fight's on" call at the 3/9 line pass. One fighter is full up, and the other fighter makes every effort to use no more than 6 Gs.

Scenario #4

Head-on pass with a "Fight's on" call when both fighters have a tally. The restricted fighter can only use pure pursuit against the full up fighter and cannot lead turn on the first pass.

Conclusion

Head-on fights are very demanding due to the maneuvering required to get to the bandit's 6 o'clock. You should think through your head-on BFM options and come up with a game plan well before you find yourself in a head-on pass with a bandit. There are no easy ways to get a shot in most head-on BFM engagements. Be patient and execute your game plan. Remember, you will win more fights if you strive to keep the jet turning at corner velocity.

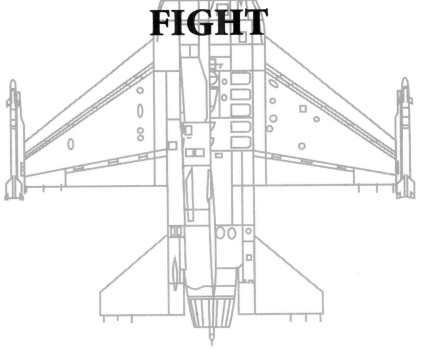

Chapter 5

INTRODUCTION TO THE BEYOND VISUAL RANGE (BVR) FIGHT

Introduction to the BVR Fight

The chapters so far in *Art of the Kill* have addressed the basic building blocks of air combat. All air combat is built on BFM—1V1 maneuvering within visual range. BFM is the first subject taught to all fighter pilots. Once a fighter pilot learns how to maneuver against targets he can see, it is time to learn to maneuver against targets that are beyond visual range (BVR). The only objective in this section of the book is to peel back the cover *slightly* on BVR air combat and expose you to the next subject area taught to fighter pilots after basic fighter maneuvers.

Modern fighters are equipped with sensors that can be used to detect targets out beyond visual range. The most common sensor used to find the enemy is the radar. When a target is found on radar, a series of tactical reactions are set in motion. These reactions to the enemy are called tactical intercepts. Tactical intercepts consist of a specific set of procedures using the radar taken by a fighter to gain an advantage on the enemy. There are six basic steps or phases to a tactical intercept. They are:

1. Detection
2. Sorting
3. Targeting
4. Intercept
5. Engage
6. Separate

A fighter pilot must understand and execute each phase. Failure to successfully execute any one of these phases will cause the breakdown of your tactical game plan. Before you fly a mission with your wingman, you should address each one of these tactical intercept phases and figure out how the flight will accomplish them.

Detection

You can't do anything until you find the enemy on your radar. At first glance, this seems straightforward. You just get pointed at the bandit, and he should appear on the scope. Not so fast. Radars have specific search volumes that are limited in elevation and azimuth. Modern fighter radars move a radar beam across 120° of azimuth as shown in Figure 5a. This sweep is called a "bar." The pilot can usually select the number of bars, up to the radar's maximum capability (usually 4 to 6 bars). In Figure 5a, the pilot has selected a 1-bar scan, while Figure 5b shows a 4-bar scan.

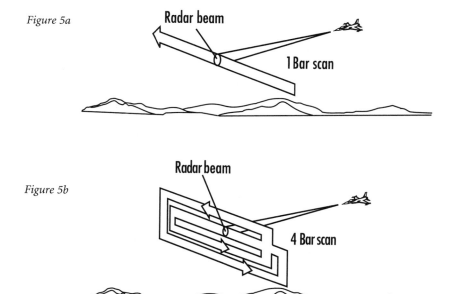

Figure 5a

Radar beam

1 Bar scan

Figure 5b

Radar beam

4 Bar scan

Each bar takes a specific amount of time for the radar to search, so it is not always advisable to select the maximum bar sweep. For example, if you know the bandits' altitude as you approached, you do not need a 4-bar scan. You can put more radar energy out there and increase your probability of detection if you scan with fewer bars. Along with selecting the bar scan, the pilot can also crank the entire search volume up or down. If the bandits are running in on the deck, you can select a 1-bar scan and crank down to search the deck for the targets. In a 1-bar scan, you are searching the area of interest faster because you are not wasting radar sweeps searching empty air space.

As you go into combat with your wingman, you should have a radar search plan. Normally, you don't want to have all the radars in the flight searching the same piece of sky. In many cases, GCI will call out targets and get you pointed at the enemy. If you know the target's altitude, then you can select a smaller elevation scan pattern (fewer bars). Most of the time, however, you will want to search the greatest volume of airspace, selecting the maximum number of bars.

GCI – ground control intercept

Sorting

Once you have detected the bandits, you must sort them. Sorting is the process of determining the following information about the enemy:

▶ How many are out there?

▶ What formation are they in?

▶ What are they doing?

As soon as each fighter in the flight completes his sort, he must pass the information to the rest of the flight. This communication serves several purposes. First, you are passing along your radar situational awareness (SA) to the other flight members, which will build their SA. Second, you are comparing radar pictures of the air battle, which helps you confirm that you are seeing what you think you are seeing. Here is an example of the radio calls during a sort.

"Falcon 1 has a two ship, line-abreast, high-aspect. South target is at angels 22. North target is at angels 20."

"Falcon 2 has a single high-aspect target at angels 22."

From this call, you can tell that number 2 has not detected one of the bandits. He knows that there is another guy out there, and he should look for him. The call by lead that the targets are at high aspect answers the "what they are doing?" question. A high aspect means that the enemy has his nose on you.

Targeting

In the targeting phase, the flight takes a specific target of responsibility. A targeting plan must be briefed before the mission and executed after the flight has sorted the enemy.

Intercept

This is the phase where you actually close on the bandit. The intercept profile is designed to get the flight into weapons parameters. Once you have targeted the bandits, it is time to drive the flight into a position to shoot. If you have BVR missiles, such as the AIM-120 AMRAAM, then you fly an intercept profile that would place you in the weapons envelope of the missile. If you only have AIM-9M Sidewinders, you fly a profile that will put you in the best position to fire these shorter-range missiles. There is one other goal of the intercept profile: in addition to driving you into weapons parameters on the bandit, your profile should keep the bandit from getting into weapons parameters on you.

Engagement

In the engagement phase, the element (your flight) enters a visual fight with the bandits. Hopefully, this will result in a brutal ambush of the enemy. Most of the time, you are not so lucky. At the same time as you find the bandits on radar, they find you. As you merge together, your element enters a maneuvering fight against the enemy formation. Element maneuvering, or ACM, is another subject—but the bottom line is fight your best 1V1 BFM. Never do anything in a two-versus-many environment that you wouldn't do in the 1V1 environment.

ACM – air combat maneuvering

Separate

Along with fighting your best BFM, you should keep in mind the position of your element in relation to your escape window. Even if you turn all the targeted bandits into scrap metal, you still need to get away from the fireball. Big, bright lights in the sky have a way of attracting attention.

Putting It All Together

The best way to show you how to perform a tactical intercept is to go through an example BVR fight from start to finish. This example will be a single F-16 (since we haven't covered two-ship tactics yet) against a two-ship of MiG-29s. The fight will start from 30 miles out at 160° of left aspect from the Fulcrums. We will assume for the sake of this discussion that no BVR missiles will be fired and the targets must be visually identified (VID).

Detection Phase

We are out there, a single ship trying to find the bad guys. Obviously the farther out we see them, the better. AWACS or GCI (ground-based radar) can help us get pointed in the right direction, but eventually we must find the bandits with our own radar in order to get a missile off the rail as soon as the bandits get within visual range. Once we get

AWACS – Airborne Warning and Control System

the targets on our radar, we need to analyze the intercept geometry to make sure we are running on the correct target. There is no need, for example, to try to run an intercept on a zero aspect target at 30 miles—we would never catch them. AWACS calls a target, and we get turned and point our radar in the right direction. Looking at the scope, we find targets at 160° left aspect at 30 miles.

The Sort/Targeting Phase

The next thing we have to do is sort the bandits. During the sort phase, we should try to determine how many bandits are out there and what formation they are flying. From the radar picture shown below in Figure 5-1, we determine that we have a two ship in line abreast formation.

Figure 5-1 Normal Acquisition Mode (NAM) Radar with Two Targets Line Abreast

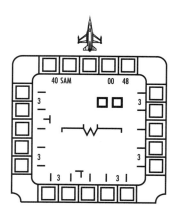

We have sorted the bandits, so now it is time to go to the targeting phase. In the targeting phase, we pick a single target and lock on to him. Since these guys are flying a visual formation, we can lock on to either guy as long as we keep in mind which one we have targeted.

The Intercept

Now we have to complete the intercept, get a VID and shoot this guy. Since we need to get a VID to shoot these bandits, the best intercept to fly is a stern conversion. By rolling out the bandit's 6 o'clock, we will have time to pick up a tally on the bandit and get a shot. If we go in at high aspect, we may not see the bandit until we are inside Rmin for a missile shot.

What is a stern conversion, you ask? A stern conversion is shown in Figure 5-2.

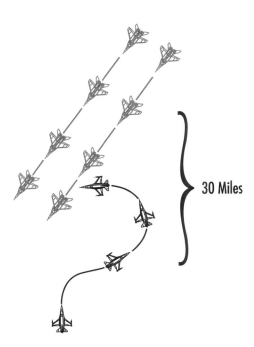

Figure 5-2 Stern Conversion Intercept

30 Miles

There are several steps to flying a stern conversion intercept.

1. Switch to SAM (Situation Awareness Mode) or STT (Single Target Track) radar mode to get the aspect angle of the bandit formation. Figure 5-3 shows a radar display with the aspect angle of the target marked.

Figure 5-3

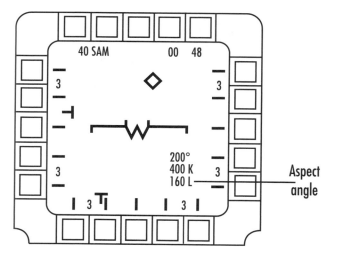

2. Turn opposite the aspect angle to get turning room on the targets. In other words, if the aspect is 160° left aspect, then you need to turn right to move the targets to the left side of the scope. **Do not turn so far that you take them off the scope.** Just turn far enough to put them about 40° on the scope. Figure 5-4 shows how you make this turn. Notice the figure has a god's-eye view and a radar view. All you are going to get in the jet is a radar view. It is up to you to use your gray matter to convert a radar display to a god's-eye view of the intercept.

Figure 5-4

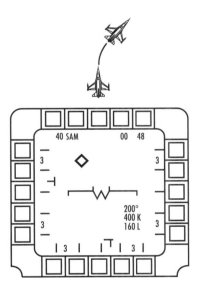

Now is a good time to show what happens if you don't analyze the aspect properly and turn the wrong way for offset. Let's say the aspect was 160° left and you turned left for offset. Would this work? The answer is no, and Figure 5-5 shows why. If you turn the wrong way, you will actually be taking away your turning room rather than increasing it. This will not be obvious by just looking at the target's position on the radar scope.

Figure 5-5

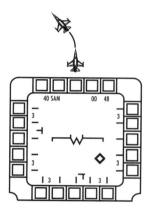

3. The next step is to hold the targets at 40° on the scope and drive in. In order to hold the targets at 40°, you may have to check turn into them occasionally. The explanation for this is a little outside the scope of this book, but put simply—a target that is not on a collision course will always drift away from you. Think about this statement in driving terms. If you are driving on a two lane highway, you will notice that the oncoming traffic moves across your windshield and then suddenly flashes by. The oncoming traffic never just stays in the exact same spot on the windshield unless you are about to end up with chrome between your teeth. The same thing applies in air combat. During an intercept, you are driving the target away from a collision angle in order to get turning room. That means that the target will keep drifting farther away from you unless you turn to hold it at a particular angle.

In order to perform an intercept, all you have to do is follow the procedures. It's just like baking a cake. You don't have to understand the chemical process, you just have to follow the steps.

4. When you get to 10 miles from the bandits, go to STT and turn to put the target you are locked to in the HUD. This is the part of the intercept where things get serious. There are two reasons that we put the target on the nose at 10 miles. The first reason is so we can get a tally on the target. In the HUD, we have a Target Designator box with a target in it. Figure 5-6 shows a HUD with the TD box labeled.

Figure 5-6

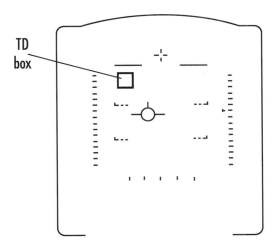

The other reason we turn to put the target on the nose at 10 miles is to get small. It is much harder to see a jet that is pointing at you because there is less surface area to look at.

When we get a tally on the target, the intercept is over and it is time to use BFM. Remember in this fight that we only have a TD box on one of the two targets. As soon as we get a tally on the bandit in the HUD, we need to look for the other guy. Don't make the mistake of putting your eyes into the "random flail" mode. If the bandits have stayed in a visual formation (which is about 90% of the time), then the other bandit will be just outside the HUD when you get a tally on the guy in the TD box.

The Engagement Phase

Now that we have two MiG-29s in sight, we must kill the one in the TD box fast and then go 1V1 with the other Fulcrum. If you can't smoke the bandit in the TD box fast, then you have to beat it. For this reason, be ready to shoot as soon as you can VID the target. Shoot and kill and, if you miss, do the "Jane Fonda routine" and give peace a chance. While you're giving peace a chance, be at high speed and high angle-off from the Fulcrums. Again, you must resist the temptation to enter a turning fight.

Let's say we do kill one of the Fulcrums at the merge—now what?

When entering a dynamic turning fight against a very maneuverable aircraft in an F-16, you need to remember one concept—lead turn. My game plan if I'm committed to stay and fight is to use a nose low slice at the pass and lead turn at every opportunity. Once you turn 180°, however, your escape window is shut and unless something strange happens (like the MiG is hit by a meteor), you must kill the bandit in order to survive the fight. In a lead turning fight, you must initiate your turn on the Fulcrum **prior** to passing his 3/9 line. In addition, strive to be at corner airspeed on the initial turn at the merge.

While you are in this lead turning fight with the Fulcrum, think weapons. A Sidewinder can fly better BFM than you can, so put one in the air if you get a chance. Keep in mind, however, that at high aspect when you are in missile parameters on the MiG-29, he may also have you in parameters for **his** missile. Again, you must fight hard because it is him or you once you enter a turning fight.

Full-on Engagement

This last narrative talks about a fight that I was in a short while back, out at Red Flag. The engagements are brief, but they illustrate how the principles of BFM are applied to accomplish the combat objectives of killing and surviving in an air battle.

A Red Flag launch is always a zoo, and this one was no exception. I had a four ship of F-16s and had gone over to the tower's ground control frequency only to be greeted on the radio with a cacophony of other flights trying to do the same thing. A few guys must have taxied late and messed up the whole flow, and once the flow of a Red Flag launch starts to go awry, it's best to just wait it out.

Red Flag is flown out of Nellis AFB just north of Las Vegas, Nevada. Nellis has two long parallel runways which helps get everybody off the ground, but you still have the problem of getting about 50 jets "quick checked" and armed. A fighter always taxis with all weapons and ordnance safed up. What that means for a training sortie is that your bombs, chaff and flares have safety pins installed to keep them from inadvertently firing. Down at the end of the runway, two separate crews get you ready for takeoff. One crew does what we call a "quick check." They look you over for air worthiness, stuff like the tread on the tires, flight control surfaces and things of this nature. The other crew arms all of your ordnance: bombs, chaff and flares. So when you have to get a big package off the ground, you have to have a taxi and arming plan.

They say that "God is in the details." The person who came up with that pearl must have tried to plan a Red Flag launch. The plan has to take into account all the "what ifs" such as what if a member of a flight has an aircraft problem and taxis late, what if someone aborts in the arming area and has to taxi back, what if the arming crews start running behind and you get gridlock on the taxiways. Something usually goes wrong, so the success of launch hinges on how everybody reacts to these "what ifs."

As I sat there turning jet fuel to noise and watched A-10s, F-16s, F-15s, Weasel F-4s, Marine F/A-18s and British Tornados lumbering past me down the taxiway, I wasn't sure what the problem was, but I knew that it was my taxi time and there was no way I could taxi. Well, I've been around long enough to know that getting stuck in the middle of dorked-up Red Flag launches has about the same probability as getting a zit on your nose on prom night—it is just inevitable. You just have to be patient and wait your turn, so that is what I did.

On this mission, my flight was flying as Red Air. As Red Air, our job was to act as Aggressors and stop Blue Air from bombing the motherland. The plan called for us to taxi behind the mass of Blue Air fighters and then arm, take off and go to our tanker that was orbiting in the western part of the Nellis ranges. Blue Air was going to take off in front of us and go to their tanker in the northeastern section of the range. I sat there and waited until everybody got past us and then finally taxied my four ship out, got quick checked, armed and took off 15 minutes late. As soon as Departure Control passed us over to Buzzsaw (the call sign for the AWACS), I asked if the war had been slipped (moved back because of the late takeoffs). Buzzsaw answered, "Negative," so right there I knew that the Moe and Curly act on the ground during the launch had cost us. I pushed the airspeed up to just below the Mach and raced for the tanker, hoping that he had extra gas.

We got our first break of the day because we were the first of the Red Air jets to get on the tanker. We were clean (no external tanks) so the tanker had the gas to top us off. Tanker drivers are the greatest. They will normally do anything for a dime and give you a nickel change. A tanker driver will fly his big jet upside down if he thinks it would help you. On this mission, the tanker guys were an Air Force Reserve unit from North Carolina flying KC-10s, and we were on and off the tanker in record time.

Unfortunately, record time still had us running four minutes late. I turned my four ship toward the east and went as fast as I could in military power. Our specific job as Red Air was to Combat Air Patrol (CAP) Tolicha Air Field. Tolicha Air Field is a target airfield out in the western section of the Nellis Ranges. It has a few aircraft hulks on the dirt taxiways and runways, and it is usually a Blue Air target. As my flight approached Tolicha, I came up on Red Air Primary frequency and asked Buzzsaw for the big picture. When AWACS has to provide information to large numbers of fighters, they normally use what we call bull's-eye control. What this means is that they call a target's position in relation to a geographical reference. Today we were using a mountain called Quartzite.

When I came up on Red Air Primary, there was a burst of noise as other Red Air flights were calling targets and starting to commit out of their CAPs. Some Red Air fighters got off the ground so late that they skipped the tanker and went straight to their CAP points. These guys were now committing on the "enemy" and executing the Red Air game plan. Our plan was to send about half our force toward the first large formation we detected and disrupt their flow before they could get going. The other half would be held in reserve in a goal-keeping role. Once the first merge occurred, the goalkeepers would commit as two ships to intercept the Blue Air players that got through the first merge.

In between all of the commotion, I heard a few bull's-eye calls from Buzzsaw that told me that a gorilla had just pushed westbound from Student Gap. A gorilla is a fighter pilot term for a large formation, usually in a close trail formation. Typically a gorilla has a minimum of six jets, arranged in some sort of visual formation with about one to two mile spacing between flights. I couldn't tell the formation from the bull's-eye calls, but I knew that it was show time. Student Gap is a saddle in a north-south oriented mountain chain on the eastern border of the Nellis Range Complex. Student Gap is easy to find, so it is frequently used by pilots as a jump-off point when running from the east to the targets in the western part of the range.

Events quickly unfolded as my four ship reached Tolicha Air Field. We did not have time to set up the full counter rotating CAP that I had briefed, so I called an audible. I told my number 3 and 4 man to spin (make a full 360° turn) over Tolicha and listen to Buzzsaw for updates. There was a possibility that the group at Student Gap was just the escort fighters and the fighters carrying bombs had not committed east yet. The whole trick to defending an area on the ground is to find the guys with the bombs and attack them, avoiding the escort fighters altogether. This is not an easy task to accomplish because when AWACS calls targets, you don't know what kind of fighters are pointing your way. If you don't go after them, they may be carrying bombs—in fact, a corollary to Murphy's Law says that if you don't commit on them, then they **will** be carrying bombs. The key is to not commit your entire force to the first big enemy formation that is detected. Always keep a few in reserve just in case you rush in there expecting to club a baby seal and end up wrestling a polar bear.

My wingman and I proceeded east and soon had multiple targets on our radar. The radio now filled with kill calls as the first Red Air flights merged with the bandits. We listened for what types of aircraft were involved. We were teamed with F/A-18s as Red Air, and so everybody else was Blue Air. The British Tornado and F-111s flying out of Canon AFB were the guys with the bombs while F-15s flew Blue Air escort. The A-10s usually trailed the big strike packages and flew Close Air Support (CAS) along the Forward Edge of the Battle Area (FEBA). All the tally calls were on F-15s. I didn't hear a single tally or kill call on a Tornado or a Vark (F-111), but by now my two ship was 10 miles from what looked to be another two ship at about 120° of right aspect. We had driven this far so it was time to stick our nose in this one and see for ourselves. When I got to five miles, I picked up a tally on two F-15s in a line abreast formation. I couldn't get my Sidewinder to lock on so I pressed in and continued to swing their 3/9 line to get behind them. Just as I got to about 50° of right aspect at 1.5 miles, they picked up a tally and broke into me. With my wingman clearing my 6 o'clock, I rolled out of my turn momentarily to drive to the entry window.

Why did I roll out, you ask? Remember from our offensive BFM discussion that we need turning room to execute a turn of our own and solve the BFM problems created by the bandit. At the point the F-15 started his turn, I did not have enough room to complete my turn so I had to roll out momentarily to get lateral displacement from the bandit and drive to the entry window. If I kept my turn coming, I would just eat up my turning room and pass the F-15 close aboard. My original turn was based on him driving in a straight line. When he turned, I had to lay some offensive BFM on him.

Where was I, oh yeah—with the trailing Eagle at 30° in the HUD and my airspeed at 450 knots, I started a classic offensive BFM engagement. I pulled 8 Gs into the F-15, and he kept his turn coming with his lift vector right on me. His wingman was out in front of him by this time and had gone high. As I fought the low F-15, my wingman called, "Stripped" and engaged the high Eagle who never even saw him. Before I could work my way in for a gun shot, my wingman got an unobserved AIM-9 shot on the high Eagle and called him dead. Meanwhile I got to 3,000 feet on the low man, pulled to lead and got a guns kill before the Eagle driver started his jink. I was now down to 280 knots and felt as vulnerable as a naked man in a sausage factory. It was time to get away from there fast before something bad happened. We were both pointing southeast as the fight ended and needed to get going west. Before turning around to west, though, I put the nose down and accelerated quickly to 450 knots. We then turned west toward Tolicha to reset in the CAP.

Why not turn at 280 knots, you ask? Remember: always turn at corner airspeed whenever you can. You are the most vulnerable in turns. Unless you are engaged defensive, it is usually best to take a few seconds to get back to corner before turning.

This is the phase in the big 50-jet fights when anything can happen. Two big groups had merged together and now there could be jets strung out anywhere along the entire 100 mile by 50 mile air combat arena. If they were uniformly distributed, it would not be a problem. Unfortunately, that's not what happens. The guys with the bombs go for their targets, and Red Air goes after them. The Blue Air escort tries to help and also ends up close to these same target areas.

In this fight, the group that pushed from Student Gap was a classic feint using all air-to-air F-15s. The

Tornados and Varks pushed about two minutes later from a point farther south with a small escort of Eagles. My second element that stayed over Tolicha had picked them up on radar. The strikers were heading for a target array in an area called Gold Flats. My second element had carved up two Tornados before getting engaged by two Eagles. All this was happening as we were heading west. Since we had to pass near Gold Flats on the way to Tolicha, we detected a big fight in that area on our radar and so we committed on this fight. We came in high, and I immediately picked up a tally on two high speed Varks at very low altitude. The sky was actually filled with jets of every description, but all I saw or cared about at the time were the two F-111s that were in my HUD. I lit the burner to close the gap and quickly accelerated to 750 knots. As I rolled out on the Varks, I noticed that I wasn't closing very fast. I looked at their airspeed displayed on my radar, and it showed they were smoking along at 650 knots. Jeez Louise, I might not have enough gas to run these guys down.

As I was contemplating this dilemma, I was being annoyed by a loud buzzing in my earphones and my wingman squawking to me about something or other. I remember thinking, "I wish everyone would just shut up so I could figure out if I had enough gas to run these Varks down." Wait a minute. "Say again, two." My wingman repeated in an exasperated tone, "Come hard left—hard left, Eagle in your deep 6 for two miles." Coming to my senses, I snapped the throttle to idle to get down to corner airspeed while simultaneously pulling the jet around in an 8 G turn looking for the bandit. I picked up a tally on a single Eagle at my 6 and expected Buzzsaw to pass a kill call on me, but Buzzsaw was quiet so I kept fighting. After about four seconds of turning at idle, I slammed the throttle back to full AB and kept my lift vector right on the Eagle. He started a big nose high move in the vertical, and so I kept my lift vector on him and went up with him.

Even if the sky is black with the enemy, you must fight the most immediate threat. I really didn't have a choice in this case but to keep my lift vector on the guy and challenge him even though it cost me knots. If I stayed level when he went up, he would have sliced down on me and drilled me.

He immediately saw that this vertical position was going to get him shot, so he pulled back down into me, and we passed canopy to canopy with about 150° of angle-off. There are two things that you need to enter a multi-bogey turning fight—situation awareness and gas. Even then, you sometimes get whacked. Without these two things, however, your odds of survival are low. So when your situation awareness and gas are low, it is best to quickly become a pacifist. As I passed the F-15 close aboard, I decided that it was time to "think thoughts of peace and not of affliction." In the separation, I looked back at the Eagle and it turned out that he didn't want to fight either so we both turned tail and accelerated in opposite directions. It was about this time that my pea brain realized that I was "blind" on my wingman—I called, "Position, two." He stated that he was engaged offensive with an Eagle above my fight. I told him that he'd better kill him quick or end up single ship because I was leaving the fight and heading westbound to the tanker. There were campers on the ground in the surrounding mountains that probably had better situation awareness on this fight than I did. It was time to get small and go fast. My wingman soon called a snapshot on the Eagle but not a kill and then fell in behind me as we headed west.

Well, another fine day at the office was near an end as we found the tanker and sucked down a couple of thousand pounds of gas. We could have made it back to Nellis without the extra gas, but it is always nice to have extra fuel when you know that there are 50 other guys heading for the same patch of concrete.

Red Air's mission would have been a resounding success but for the fact that we didn't have CAP far enough forward to get to the bombers before they dropped their bombs. The Varks and the Tornado did not get "tapped" until they were *off* the target, and Buzzsaw was a little slow communicating the presence of the second (and more important) gorilla.

From a BFM standpoint, a lot of F-15s got shot while doing a great job protecting the bombers. My element did well, getting several kills and surviving the engagement.

Conclusion

Art of the Kill has provided a solid introduction to Basic Fighter Maneuvers, following the normal progression of the air-to-air phase of fighter training:

▶ BFM Geometry

▶ Offensive BFM

▶ Defensive BFM

▶ Head-on BFM

It also provided a brief overview of the next two subjects taught in a fighter curriculum:

▶ Intercept Geometry

▶ Tactical Intercepts

Fighter pilot instructors use this "building block" approach to teach fundamental fighter pilot skills. Without BFM, a fighter pilot cannot master any other phase of air combat. Now that you have a solid BFM foundation, you should be ready to move on to the more advanced air combat subjects.

Until then, fly hard and shoot straight.

Afterword

Art of the Kill and "Fighter Air Combat Trainer" provided a solid introduction to Basic Fighter Maneuvers. The next in the *Art of the Kill* series will expand the coverage of BVR combat tactics and maneuvering, and will include tactics for maneuvering "elements" and "flights" of two or more aircraft against multiple opponents.

The third in this series will take a unique perspective—that of the world-class "adversary" aircraft the MiG-29 Fulcrum. Flown by very few Western pilots, the MiG-29's unique flight dynamics and weapons suite make flying and fighting from its cockpit a unique art.

Those of you who are interested in further reading on the subject of modern air combat may wish to read *Fighter Combat: Tactics and Maneuvering* by Robert Shaw (Naval Institute Press) and *The Ace Factor: Air Combat and the Role of Situational Awareness* by Mike Spick (Naval Institute Press).

BFM LESSON PLANS

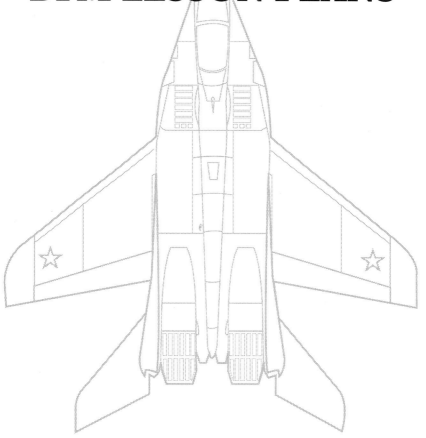

BFM Lesson Plans

This section outlines how to use *Art of the Kill* the same way a fighter pilot would use an Air Force workbook. Each chapter corresponds to a lesson, complete with lesson objectives and quizzes to test your understanding. The answer key for the quizzes is at the end of the section.

Lesson 1: Geometry of Air Combat

This lesson is designed to introduce you to the basic terms and definitions of air combat. Terms and definitions are important to understand because they will form the foundation of our discussion of Basic Fighter Maneuvers. In this section, we will describe the angular relationships between aircraft in a fight, the pursuit options, and the weapons envelope.

Objectives

Once you've read Chapter 1, you should be able to do the following:

▶ Describe the geometry of 1V1 air combat

  ▷ Identify the angular relationship between two aircraft

  ▷ Understand aspect angle

▶ Describe the attack pursuit courses

  ▷ Understand what each pursuit course offers to the attacking aircraft

  ▷ Understand how out-of-plane maneuvering affects the pursuit course

▶ Describe the weapons envelope

  ▷ Define Rmax and Rmin

  ▷ Describe the factors that affect Rmax and Rmin

Lesson 1 Quiz

1. **Which attack pursuit course is used most of the time to shoot a missile at an adversary? Holding your nose on this pursuit course for the entire attack will probably result in an overshoot.**

   a. Lag pursuit.
   b. Pure pursuit.
   c. Lead pursuit.

2. **During an out-of-plane pull away from the bandit, which attack pursuit course are you are flying?**

   a. Lag pursuit.
   b. Pure pursuit.
   c. Lead pursuit.

3. **If you place your HUD flight path marker directly on the bandit, which attack pursuit course are you flying?**

   a. Lag pursuit.
   b. Pure pursuit.
   c. Lead pursuit.

4. **You are entering gun parameters. Which attack pursuit course is necessary for a gun shot?**

   a. Lag pursuit.
   b. Pure pursuit.
   c. Lead pursuit.

5. **If you drive in on the bandit and he is able to out-turn you as you get in closer, which attack pursuit course will you more than likely get stuck in?**

   a. Lag pursuit.
   b. Pure pursuit.
   c. Lead pursuit.

6. **In question 5, the bandit is out-turning you. If this happens, where would your HUD flight path marker end up?**

a. Out in front of the bandit.
b. Directly on the bandit's jet.
c. Behind the bandit.

7. **Which positional geometry parameter do you get when you take the velocity vectors of two aircraft and measure the angle between them?**

a. Aspect angle.
b. Angle-off.
c. Collision antenna train angle.

8. **Which positional geometry parameter do you get when you take a measure in degrees from the tail of the target to your aircraft?**

a. Aspect angle.
b. Angle-off.
c. Collision antenna train angle.

9. **You are at 6 o'clock on a bandit, and he turns at high G into you. How will this hard turn by the bandit affect your missile shot?**

a. Rmax (maximum range) will move out from the aircraft, and so will Rmin (minimum range). Rmin moving out may jam your missile shot.
b. Rmin will move in, and so will Rmax. Rmin moving in will give you more time to take your shot.
c. The weapons envelope is unaffected by target G.

10. **What is the effect of target G on the Rmin for a gun shot?**

a. Moves Rmin out.
b. Moves Rmax in.
c. The gun is an all-aspect weapon that has no minimum range.

Lesson 2: Offensive BFM

Lesson 2 is designed to teach you the fundamentals of modern air combat offensive BFM. Offensive BFM is used by fighter pilots to stay behind a turning bandit and employ weapons. At first glance, this seems like a rather simple objective to accomplish. Starting behind a bandit should be easier than starting with the bandit behind you. Unfortunately, this is not the case. Offensive BFM is more complex than defensive BFM, and proficiency in offensive BFM is more difficult to achieve than any other phase of 1V1 maneuvering. The good news is that once you understand maneuvering from the offensive position, you will have solved a big piece of the air combat puzzle.

Objectives

After you've read Chapter 2, you should be able to do the following:

▶ Describe the mechanics of BFM

   ▷ Understand turn rate and radius

   ▷ Understand vertical turns

▶ Describe the concept of turning room

   ▷ Define the turn circle

   ▷ Describe lateral or horizontal turning room

   ▷ Describe vertical turning room

▶ Describe how to solve offensive BFM problems

   ▷ Determine whether a fighter is inside or outside a bandit's turn circle

   ▷ Identify the offensive BFM entry window

   ▷ Describe the procedures for getting to the elbow (also called the "control position")

▶ Describe the procedures for taking a gun shot

Lesson 2 Quiz

1. **What is the effect of airspeed on turn radius at a constant G?**

a. The faster the airspeed, the smaller the turn radius.
b. The faster the airspeed, the larger the turn radius.
c. You can't tell because it depends on the aircraft type.

2. **What is the effect of being either below or above corner velocity on turn rate?**

a. Turn rate will go down.
b. Turn rate will go down until you get to corner velocity, and then it will stay the same.
c. Again, it just depends on what kind of jet you are flying.

3. **You have entered a turning fight with a MiG-29 and are pulling 9 Gs in a level turn. You suddenly notice that your nose is not moving at the rate that it should be for this G load. What should you do?**

a. Speed up, you are too slow.
b. Slow down, you are too fast.
c. You are probably experiencing a failure in the pitch axis of the flight control computer. Eject and sort out the problem on the ground.

4. **You have just jumped a bandit, and the range in your HUD shows 1 nm. You fire an AIM-9M, but it is a shark killer and dives for the water below. The bandit, a MiG-29, gets a tally on you and takes this attack personally. In response, he pulls max Gs to jam your next missile shot. What should you do in this situation?**

a. Start an immediate climb to get turning room.
b. Drive all the way into the bandit in pure pursuit to intimidate him.
c. Drive to the position in the sky where the bandit started his turn. This will put you in the entry window.

5. In the situation in question 4, what is the best way to get turning room against this high G bandit?

a. In the vertical. You can never go wrong climbing above a hard turning bandit.

b. Drive to where the fight started, and you will gain horizontal turning room inside the bandit's turn. In a 1 nm setup, the bandit will not usually be able to take away or use your horizontal turning room inside his turn.

c. Turning room is not important in this situation because you are at 1 mile. Almost anything you do will work.

6. Which statement about vertical turns is correct?

a. When you pull your nose towards the ground, turn rate and radius increase.

b. When you pull your nose towards the ground, turn rate increases and radius decreases.

c. Gravity's effect on the turn rate and radius of high G aircraft is negligible.

7. You roll out of a tactical intercept at 2 nm behind a MiG-29. He sees you immediately and dispenses flares, while breaking into you at 8 Gs at corner velocity. Which of the following statements is true?

a. Since an immediate climb will always work, start a pull up in the vertical.

b. A high speed wiffer-shnauntz can be used to decrease aspect and angle-off in this situation.

c. You are outside the bandit's turn circle. Prepare to fly a head-on BFM fight. Any big moves for turning room may cost you.

8. **You are feeling kind of stupid, so you point your nose toward a multi-bogey fight and notice that a MiG-29 has spit out of the fight. As you approach the spitter, he sees you and starts dropping flares while turning into you. You are at 2 nm and notice that he is not generating very many angles on you. What should you do?**

a. Do the same thing that you did in the question 7. A MiG-29 at 2 nm is a MiG-29 at 2 nm, so the same thing should work.

b. Fight what you see. The MiG probably got slow in the "food fight." You are inside his turn circle. Drive for the entry window.

c. It's a trap. Separate from the fight before it is too late.

9. **How do you know when you have entered the offensive BFM entry window?**

a. The range decreases to 4,500 feet.

b. When the bandit is 30° off your nose, you are inside the entry window and can start your turn.

c. The entry window light in the cockpit flashes.

10. **At what range from the bandit should you normally go from lag to lead pursuit in offensive BFM?**

a. 3,000 feet.

b. 4,500 feet.

c. Exact procedures do not apply to modern air combat. Every situation is different, so do what feels right.

Lesson 3: Defensive BFM

Defensive BFM is simple in concept. From an academic perspective, it is far simpler than offensive BFM. When a bandit shows up at your 6 o'clock, you simply create BFM problems. In Chapter 2, we discussed solving the BFM problems of aspect angle, angle-off and range. In this lesson, we will talk about creating these exact same BFM problems for an attacking bandit. We will also discuss what to do after we put some defensive BFM on the bandit and he makes offensive BFM mistakes. The theory of defensive BFM is straightforward, but in the cockpit of modern fighters, the execution is difficult. Defensive BFM requires physical strength and endurance to pull high G loads while keeping track of a bandit at 6 o'clock. This lesson will build your academic foundation in defensive BFM.

Objectives

Once you've read Chapter 3, you should be able to do the following:

▶ Describe the three ways used to detect an attacking bandit

▶ Understand the use of aspect in defending against a missile attack

▶ Understand how to create BFM problems for an attacking bandit

  ▷ Describe the procedures for executing a defensive turn

  ▷ Describe the visual cues that tell you when your defensive turn is working

▶ Describe the procedures for defending against a gun shot

Lesson 3 Quiz

1. **Your wingman calls for you to break left, and as you rack the jet around in a 7 G turn in response to his call, you see the smoke trail of the missile pulling lead on you. What should you do?**

   a. Turn to put the missile on the beam (on your 3/9 line) immediately, while dropping chaff and flares.
   b. Split-S to face the missile head-on from low altitude, dropping chaff and flares.
   c. Just keep your high-G turn coming all the way into the missile, while dropping chaff and flares.

2. **You are attempting to separate from a mature engagement above the Mach, but you don't quite make it. A MiG-29 fires a missile your way, and you decide not to bet your life that he is out of range. How should you turn to defeat this missile?**

   a. Keep your Mach up as you turn. You can never have too much airspeed.
   b. You must slow down quickly to corner velocity so you can turn at your best turn rate.
   c. Slow down to the minimum airspeed possible while turning. This will give you the tightest turn radius, which may cause the missile to overshoot.

3. **Which statement is true concerning defensive turns?**

   a. Always put your lift vector below the horizon to preserve energy.
   b. Always turn level with the horizon. That way you won't get disoriented.
   c. Don't worry about the horizon. Put your lift vector directly on the bandit during a defensive turn. If you do anything else, you will give the bandit turning room.

4. **You get a tally on a MiG-29 at 7 o'clock at over 2 nm and closing. You crank into an 8 G defensive turn, and as you come around, you notice that the bandit is not moving forward toward your 3/9 line. He is maintaining his 7 o'clock position. Given that your initial range estimation is correct, what is the problem?**

   a. This guy is very good and must know a lot about offensive BFM.
   b. You are probably too fast and are not generating your best turn rate. The bandit, therefore, is inside your turn circle and is matching your very poor turn rate.
   c. Speed up. Your turn radius is too tight.

5. **In the situation in question 4, what will normally happen when you execute the correct defensive turn into a bandit at 2 nm?**

   a. You will the drive the bandit forward toward your 3/9 line.
   b. Anything can happen in an air-to-air engagement. You just don't know what to expect.
   c. The bandit will be forced into a vertical move to maintain his position.

6. **You have gotten slow gunning a MiG-29, and as you come off the kill, you see another MiG-29 closing from 6 o'clock at 2 nm. You have only 300 knots. What should you do?**

   a. Unload the jet and accelerate to corner velocity as quickly as possible. After reaching corner, break into the MiG.
   b. Turn with all you've got before the MiG gets to your turn circle. This will give him the most BFM problems.
   c. Pray for divine intervention. It is the only thing that can work in this situation.

7. **A MiG-29 rolls out at your 6 o'clock at 1 nm. You put your best defensive turn on him, and he immediately pulls up into the vertical. What should you do?**

   a. Quake with fear. This is the dreaded high yo-yo maneuver. You are in for a real tussle.
   b. You are in luck. The bandit has just given you turning room you can use. Rotate your lift vector up into the bandit and make him pay for this buffoonery.

c. Slice for the deck to keep his nose out of phase. This is the only counter to a vertical move by the bandit.

8. **This situation is the same as in question 7, but this time, the MiG keeps his nose on you all the way in. No missiles are fired. What does this pure pursuit course tell you about the bandit?**

a. He is flying HUD BFM. He will arrive close to your jet with no turning room and will overshoot.
b. He is doing perfect BFM. Get ready for the bandit to saddle up on you for a stabilized tracking gun shot.
c. The nose position of an attacking bandit is irrelevant. You can never really tell what people are going to do, especially in high pressure situations like this one.

9. **A MiG-29 rolls out behind you at 1 nm, and as you break into him, he puts his nose in lead pursuit and closes the range. At 3,000 feet, you see that he will overshoot with his nose in lead. What should you do?**

a. The MiG is probably lining up for a snapshot. Break immediately out of plane to trash his shot.
b. Keep your lift vector on the MiG and keep pulling.
c. Ease off to 1 G to force a larger overshoot.

10. **A MiG-29 is camped at your 6 o'clock, inside gun range, with his overtake and angle-off under control. What should you do?**

a. Break straight into the bandit with your lift vector right on him to create BFM problems for him.
b. Turn into him while simultaneously dropping the gear and opening the speed brakes. This move, made famous in the movies, will always cause the bandit to overshoot.
c. Execute your planned guns jink immediately. You must start by moving out of the bandit's plane of motion. Don't expect miracles. Just keep jinking to stay alive.

Lesson 4: Head-on BFM

There is no such thing as a neutral fight. Unless you are fighting your clone in the same type of jet, the fight is not neutral. This lesson will teach you the fundamentals of fighting head-on, or high-aspect, BFM. As you approach a bandit head-on, you are certain of one thing—a great deal of maneuvering is required in order to turn this high aspect pass into a kill. Maneuvering requires energy, so in most fights that start head-on, you will normally get lower and slower as the fight progresses. This lesson will teach you how to spend your energy smartly so that you can efficiently maneuver for a kill once you enter a head-on fight.

Objectives

After you've read Chapter 4, you should be able to do the following:

▶ Understand the concept of the escape window

▶ Describe the factors that affect your decision to stay and fight or to separate

▶ Understand the concept of the lead turn

▶ Describe the options at the pass

   ▷ Identify the advantages and disadvantages of nose-low, level and vertical turns

   ▷ Understand the concept of over-the-top airspeed and how it is used to fight in the vertical

▶ Understand basic head-on BFM geometry

   ▷ Describe the advantages and disadvantages of a one-circle fight

   ▷ Describe the advantages and disadvantages of a two-circle fight

Lesson 4 Quiz

1. **You have entered a head-on fight with a MiG-29, and after the third pass, you find yourself in a Lufbery. You are stagnated directly across a 2,000 foot circle with neither fighter able to gain on the other. Where is your escape window in this situation?**

   a. Your escape window is open because your angle-off is high. At any time, you can roll wings-level and accelerate out of the fight.
   b. Your escape window is closed because you are at low energy. If you try to roll out and separate, the bandit will continue his turn and spank you like a baby.
   c. The escape window is both open and closed. It depends on how good you are at accelerating the jet. A skillful pilot can always get out of a turning fight.

2. **You have entered an offensive fight against a MiG-29 and are inside his turn circle in a perfect lag position, about to go lead for guns. Suddenly your bingo warning (low fuel) sounds and Betty (the voice warning system) reminds you that it is time to get out of Dodge. What are your options?**

   a. You should keep turning and kill this guy. Your escape window is shut, and the only way out of this one is through a cloud of enemy hair, teeth, and eyeballs.
   b. Since you are on the offensive, your escape window is open. You are low on gas, so dive out of your escape window and separate from the fight.
   c. This is a complex situation. You should stay in lag and think it over. Flying fighters is a very intellectual endeavor that, at times, requires a pause for quiet contemplation.

3. **You have just come off a kill and are accelerating the jet away to distance yourself from the fireball. As you check 12 o'clock, you pick up a tally on a MiG-29 two miles off your nose, turning toward your jet. What are your options?**

   a. You must turn and enter a fight with this guy. Your escape window is closed because the MiG-29 has a tally.
   b. You can enter a head-on BFM engagement with this guy or separate. All your options are open.
   c. An immediate pull into the vertical in this situation will usually work.

4. **You are committed to a head-on fight. Which statement is true concerning lead turns?**

a. Lead turns should only be made in the horizontal.
b. When fighting head-on, you should always attempt to lead turn. Lead turns are the most efficient way to trade energy for position.
c. Lead turns should only be used if you have a jet that can out-turn the enemy.

5. **You are approaching a head-on pass with a MiG-29 and have decided to stay and fight. Your game plan is to execute a slicing lead turn. Which statement is true when using a slicing lead turn game plan?**

a. The slice should be executed at corner velocity, with your nose about 10° low.
b. The biggest advantage of the slice is that it is the best move you can make to keep a tally.
c. A slice should be made as slow as possible to shrink your turn radius.

6. **You executed a slice into a MiG-29 after a head-on pass, and he rolled away from you, put his lift vector on you, and started pulling. What can you expect from this fight?**

a. Since you pulled into him and he rolled away from you at pass, you have entered a two-circle fight. You may have a chance for a front aspect AIM-9M.
b. The bandit will make angles on you because turning away from the other fighter on a head-on pass is the best way to execute a lead turn.
c. You should have some angles on the bandit, since he turned away and gave you turning room. This is a one-circle fight, and you will probably be in too tight for an AIM-9M shot.

7. **After passing a MiG-29 head-on, you enter a 7 G level turn into the bandit. Which statement is true concerning the level turn option at the pass?**

a. You can get your nose around faster by doing a level turn than you can by using any other head-on BFM option.
b. Level turns are not very efficient BFM, but you can usually maintain a tally during a level turn and it is easy to execute a level turn. (This is important because most head-on engagements are lost and not won.)

   c. One of the disadvantages of doing a level turn at the pass is that you will probably lose sight of the bandit.

8. You are about to pass head-on with a bandit but find yourself above him. As you close on the bandit, he is nose-high and you are nose-low. What will the bandit probably do, and how do you counter it?

   a. The bandit is in a perfect position for a nose-high-to-nose-low lead turn. Any time you pass a bandit who is coming uphill into you at high angles, you must counter the big lead turn with a lead turn of your own.

   b. The bandit's best move is to pass you and keep climbing for an altitude advantage. To counter the bandit's move in the vertical, extend downhill until you get to corner velocity and then zoom.

   c. The bandit is in a bad position to enter a head-on fight in this situation, so turn away from him to force a one-circle fight.

9. Which statement is true about pulling up in the vertical during a head-on fight?

   a. All pulls in the vertical should be done at corner velocity or above. This may require you to extend for energy after passing the bandit.

   b. Always start your pull in the vertical with your lift vector oriented toward the bandit. This will normally cause you to pull up in the oblique on your initial move.

   c. Normally, it is best to make your initial pull into the vertical from a wings-level position. After reaching the 90° point in your pull, roll and put your lift vector on the bandit.

10. You have merged with a MiG-29 and entered a two-circle fight. You are winchester (out of missiles). What is your primary concern in this fight as you pull around for your second pass with the bandit?

   a. Sometimes you have a chance to shoot an all-aspect heat missile in a two-circle fight. You don't have a missile, and he does, so "Heads up."

   b. You should only think in terms of lead turning the bandit in this situation, since two-circle fights are always too tight for a missile shot.

   c. Since two-circle fights are inherently tighter than one-circle fights, be prepared to enter a scissors.

Answer Key to Quizzes

Lesson 1: Geometry	Lesson 2: Offensive	Lesson 3: Defensive	Lesson 4: Head-on
1. b	1. b	1. a	1. b
2. a	2. a	2. b	2. a
3. b	3. b	3. c	3. b
4. c	4. c	4. b	4. b
5. a	5. b	5. a	5. a
6. c	6. b	6. b	6. c
7. b	7. c	7. b	7. b
8. a	8. b	8. a	8. a
9. a	9. b	9. a	9. c
10. c	10. a	10. c	10. a

Introduction

On June 2, 1972, at approximately 1330 hours, Brenda 01 (a hard-wing F-4E, tail number 68210, flown by Major Phil Handley) shot down a MiG-19 with 20mm cannon fire, approximately 30 miles northeast of Hanoi. At the time of the kill, the estimated flight parameters were: F-4 speed over Mach 1.2 (800 kts); MiG-19 speed Mach 0.77 (500 kts); altitude above terrain 500 feet; slant range 200–300 feet; and flight path crossing angle 90°. This was the only MiG-19 shot down by cannon fire during the course of the war in Southeast Asia and is believed to be the highest speed gun kill in the history of aerial combat.

F-4E Gun Kill of MiG-19 in Vietnam

Brenda, a flight of four F-4Es was on CAP north of Hanoi (axis approximately NE/SW) between the Gia Lam and Kep airfields.

> *CAP – Combat Air Patrol.*

While doing a cross turn at the south end of the CAP orbit, Brenda turned into a fake SAM launch.

> *Cross turn – A 180° turn in which the two elements of the four-ship flight turned toward each other.*

> *Fake SAM launch – A SAM operator "electronically simulated" a missile launch to force a defensive reaction by Brenda Flight.*

At this time, the element Brenda 03 became separated, hit Bingo and began egress to the east.

> *Element – Two aircraft operating as a tactical unit within a flight of four or more aircraft.*

> *Bingo – Pilot jargon for running low on fuel. A plane with Bingo fuel has enough to get back to base safely, but not much more.*

At approximately the same time, two MiGs launched from the Gia Lam airport to intercept the Brenda 01 element and were called out to Brenda 01 by "Worm," Brenda's controller on the Red Crown frequency.

> **Controller** – *A ground- or ship-based controller who uses radar to keep pilots advised of the tactical situation.*
>
> **Red Crown** – *The control agency aboard a U.S. Navy cruiser located in the Gulf of Tonkin.*

Brenda 01 turned to meet them, but Brenda 02 called Bingo.

Brenda 01 and 02 then began egress on a heading of 100° at approximately 15,000 and 500 KCAS with Brenda 02 on the right side, 1,000 feet out, line abreast.

> **Line abreast** – *A tactical formation in which both planes fly even with each other.*

During this egress, Brenda 01 caught a sun flash through the scattered cloud deck at approximately 10,000 feet and 3 o'clock position and erroneously called it out as a MiG-21 while crossing Brenda 02 to the left wing.

Brenda 01 continued to look in vain for several seconds with no results until a weak golf-band one-ringer at 4 o'clock on his RHAW caused Brenda 01 to scan further aft, where he saw two silver MiG-19s in sharp bearing formation, closing on him in a curve of pursuit from his 4 to 5 o'clock position.

> **Golf-band one-ringer** – *A weak radar signal (extending to only the first concentric circle of the RHAW scope) in the G-band frequency range.*
>
> **RHAW** – *Radar Homing And Warning set.*
>
> **Sharp bearing formation** – *The second MiG-19 is flying 30°–45° and 200–400 feet off the lead plane's tail.*

Telling Brenda 02 to continue the egress while he engaged, Brenda 01, in full afterburner, did a very high G 135° slice into the attacking element.

Brenda 01 felt the F-4 go supersonic after approximately 90° of turn.

> **Supersonic** –*Faster than the speed of sound. (In the F-4, the pilot can feel the aerodynamic shift of the center of lift on the wing as the Mach is breached.)*

The MiG-19s, instead of continuing their attack to pass Brenda 01 close aboard to deny him turning room, initially turned down and left to a heading of approximately south.

At no time during the slice turn did Brenda 01 take his eyes off the MiGs.

However, by the 300° point of Brenda 01's turn, he found himself exactly "tail on" to the tiny MiGs at a range of approximately two miles… at which point they simply disappeared before Brenda 01's 20:10 eyes.

Brenda 01 then let off the G to lag to the outside of the perceived turn circle and almost immediately picked up the MiGs again as they began to show some planform view due to their continuing right, descending turn.

> *Planform* – *Top view.*

Pulling the nose to pure pursuit, Brenda 01 asked for and got 5 mile boresight.

> *Pure pursuit* – *Nose of your aircraft pointed directly at the target.*

> *5 mile boresight* – *A radar and HUD symbology setting. The pilot, Handley, asked his backseater, Smallwood, for the desired setting.*

With the pipper on the trailing MiG, an "auto acquisition" radar lock-on was achieved.

After four seconds of settling time, Brenda 01 ripple fired his two AIM-7 Sparrows.

> *Settling time* – *Time allowed for the radar and missile circuits to settle to a stable lock-on.*

> *Ripple fired* – *Fired multiple weapons at once in the hope that one would reach the target.*

The first missile's rocket motor did not ignite, and the second failed to guide.

The MiG leader, apparently seeing the smoke trail from the second AIM-7, tightened his turn greatly, turning both MiGs in balls of condensation in the humid SEA air.

> **SEA** – *Southeast Asia.*

Seeing this, Brenda did a lag pursuit roll to reduce angle-off as he selected heat missiles.

> **Lag pursuit** – *A roll to the outside of the turn to reduce angle-off.*

> **Angle-off** – *The difference in nose direction between two aircraft.*

> **Heat missiles** – *A heat-seeking (infrared-guided) missile.*

Brenda 01 got the standard AIM-4 background tone, heard it rise to tracking tone as he put his pipper on the trailing MiG, uncaged the missile heads, pulled lead, and ripple fired his two remaining AIM-4E missiles.

> **AIM-4** – *An early generation of infrared-guided missile.*

> **Uncaged** – *Enabling the missile seeker head to independently track the target after lock-on.*

The first missile went ballistic, and the second never left the right inboard pylon launcher rail.

> **Ballistic** – *The missile failed to track its target, flying as straight as a bullet instead.*

By now, the fight had descended to approximately 500 feet AGL, and the slant range from Brenda 01 to the MiGs (which were still in very close bearing formation) was decreasing very fast from about 3,000 feet, with an angle-off rapidly approaching 90°.

> **Slant range** –*The straight line distance between the two aircraft.*

Brenda 01 selected guns, pulled his nose into lead pursuit (carrying the trailing MiG in the left quarter panel of his windscreen so he could keep him in sight), and at the last moment, rolled slightly left and up into the plane of motion, and held down the trigger.

Once in the plane of motion, Brenda 01 was unable to see the MiG due to the long nose of the F-4E, but shortly thereafter the trailing MiG flew squarely through Brenda 01's plane of turn at a slant range of 200–300 feet and 90°–100° angle-off, at which time he saw multiple 20mm hits down the axis of the MiG.

Brenda 01 quarter-rolled and zoomed and continued to watch the MiG, which was now in heavy wing rock, nose dropping, with fire, pieces of the aircraft and fluids streaming from the right wing root.

>   ***Zoomed*** – *Traded speed for altitude.*

The MiG's nose continued to drop and it crashed almost vertically into a green meadow, exploding in a huge orange ball of fire, approximately 10 seconds after Brenda 01's 300 round burst.

Brenda 01's quarter roll and zoom maneuver terminated with a hard pull down from vertical to horizontal flight to a heading of east, at an altitude of over 15,000, with an indicated airspeed still something in excess of 700 knots.

F-4E

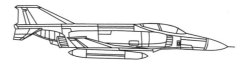

Flight Parameters	1	1A	2	3	3A	4	5
Airspeed (indicated)	450	550	722	751	N/A	818	818
Altitude (feet)	15,000	10,000	5,000	3,000	N/A	500	500
Bank (degrees)	0	135	60	75	N/A	82	82
Average G during Turn	N/A	7	2	4	N/A	7	7
True Airspeed (knots)	565	640	780	785	N/A	825	825
Mach Number	0.9	1.0	1.2	1.2	N/A	1.25	1.25
Horizontal Turn Radius (feet)	N/A	3,400	26,400	1,400	N/A	9,800	9,800

MiG-19

Flight Parameters	1	1A	2	3	3A	4	5
Airspeed (indicated)	585	602	602	629	620	596	500
Altitude (feet)	5,000	5,000	5,000	3,000	1,000	500	500
Bank (degrees)	80	N/A	60	N/A	83	83	83
Average G during Turn	6	N/A	2	N/A	8	8	8
True Airspeed (knots)	631	650	650	655	632	601	504
Mach Number	0.97	1.0	1.0	1.0	0.96	0.91	0.77
Horizontal Turn Radius (feet)	5,700	N/A	18,000	N/A	4,400	3,900	2,800

Top View

Side View

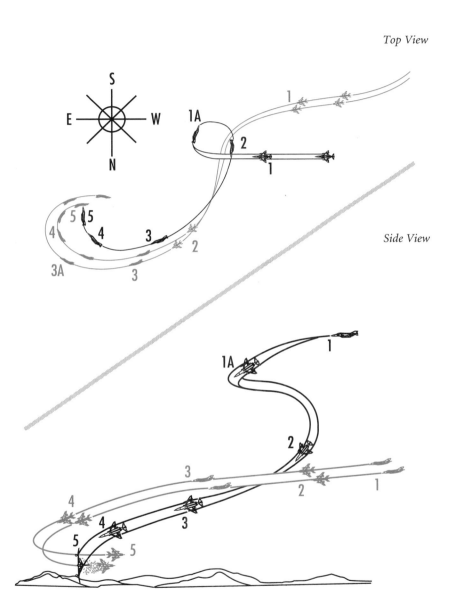

Radio Transcript

Brenda Flight
> Brenda 01: Handley and Smallwood
> Brenda 02: Green and Eden
> Brenda 03: Downey and Leach
> Brenda 04: Ellis and White

Other Players
> Red Crown: control agency from U.S. Navy cruiser in gulf
> Worm: controller on Red Crown
> Tea Ball: "black" (highly classified) control agency
> Fletch: another F-4 MiG CAP in the area
> Milo: photo reconnaissance flight

Mission Tape

Time: 0+00
> Handley: "Brenda, reverse."

Time: 0+07
> E-SAM high tone
> Handley: "Brenda has the E-SAM high."

> > *E-SAM high tone – There are typically four phases to the firing of an SA-2 missile. 1) When the SA-2 SAM radar operator first acquires lock-on (E-SAM low), the F-4 RHAW will emit a soft "chirping" tone that sounds like a rattlesnake. 2) As the operator refines his lock-on and increases his power and pulse recurring frequency (PRF), the F-4 RHAW tone increases in pitch and volume (E-SAM high). 3) When the SA-2 is launched, the F-4 RHAW emits a piercing, solid, 1,000Hz tone and illuminates a large red warning light in the cockpit that says, "LAUNCH." 4) As the SA-2 (now in flight) begins to receive command guidance signals from the controlling radar (triplicate movement), the RHAW illuminates a second cockpit warning light that is yellow and is labeled "A. S.," which stands for Azimuth Sector. (However, most pilots referred to this light as the "Ah Shit" light, for it definitely meant that you were the target.)*

Time: 0+21
    1000Hz launch tone
        Handley: "Launch."
        Smallwood: "Launch."
        Handley: "OK, we've got a launch light… Brenda, let's turn into it…"

Time: 0+30
    "Fletch, this is Bing. You have a possible bandit 058 Bull's-eye 15."

Time: 0+35
    Handley: "Brenda, pods on."
        Handley: "I don't see that fucker."
        Smallwood: "I don't either."
        Downey: "Brenda, 3's going to turn eastbound… I lost you in that break."
        Handley: "OK, Brenda, let's reverse course back to east."

       Pod *– ECM pod.*

Time: 0+57
    Tea Ball: "[garble]… Bull's-eye… 060, 20 nautical."
        Red Crown: "Brenda, Worm… Bandit will be on your 167 at 8… possible 167 at 8."
        Handley: "Copy that."
        Handley: "OK, ten thousand pounds."
        Downey: "[garble]… Brenda 4… Roger… [garble]"

Time: 1+20
    Red Crown: "Brenda, you're in the dark, bandit 047 Bull's-eye 14."
        Handley: "Roger."
        Downey: "Brenda 4, copy, blower."

       Blower *– Pilot slang for afterburner.*

Time: 1+38
Handley: "Red Crown, Brenda 1, where's the bandit?"
Green: "Brenda 2's bingo."
Red Crown: "Stand by, you're in the dark, estimate…"
Handley: "OK, give me egress heading."
Unknown flight: "You've got friendlies up there to the left, boys."

Time: 1+48
Red Crown: "Brenda, this is Worm. Estimating the bandit 039…
[garble]"
Green: "Brenda 2 is bingo."
Handley: "OK, 2, Bre… let's bug out… bug out."
Downey: [garble]

Time: 2+06
Handley: "Turn the pod off."
AAA RHAW tone
Handley: "Pod off."
Smallwood: "It's off."
Handley: "'Off' I mean."
Smallwood: "It's off, we need about a zero nine zero… uh, one zero
zero."
Handley: "One zero zero, roger."

Time: 2+21
Ellis: "Brenda 4's bingo."
Downey: "OK, Brenda and stay line abreast… [garble]"
Ellis: "Brenda 4."
Unknown flight: "Take it around to the right."

Time: 2+30
E-SAM high tone
Unknown flight: "Jay, check my 6 o'clock back there."
Unknown flight member: "Rog, we've got two F-4s going back
there."
Unknown flight leader: "All right."
Downey: "Brenda 4, move it up line abreast."

Time: 2+40
    Handley: "OK, Fletch, Brenda is coming out."
    Fletch leader: "Roger, we're on station."
        AAA RHAW tone
        Downey: "Move it out another thousand feet, Brenda 4."
        Ellis: "OK."
    Multiple AAA and SAM RHAW tones
        Unknown flight: "Bingo."

Time: 3+15
    Smallwood: "E-SAM high at five."
        Handley: "Roger."

Time: 3+19
    Handley: "OK, I've got a MiG-21 at our 3 o'clock down there, Brenda 2… cross to the other wing; he may try to pop up on us."
        Green: "Roger."
        Faint golf-band one ring strobe at 4 o'clock, moving aft
        Handley: "We've got 95 fuel."
        Smallwood: "Roger."

Time: 3+40
    Handley: "OK, I'm going to take one quick run at him. 2, you continue on out…"
        Green: "I'll stay with you."
        Unknown: "Brenda 1… [garble]"
        Unknown: "Was that Brenda 1 exiting the area?"
        Handley: "Negative, Brenda 1's on a MiG-19."

Time: 4+02
    Handley: "Give me 5 mile boresight."
        Garbled transmissions, RHAW tones, Smallwood straining against G forces
        Smallwood: "You've got it."
        Milo flight: "Milo 2's on."
        Handley: "Fucker won't fire… there it goes."
    Garbled transmissions

Time: 4+21
    Handley: "OK, I'm going heat."
        Smallwood: "OK."
    Green: "It went ballistic, lead."
        AIM-4E select tone
        Unknown: "Say again."
        Unknown: "Say your position, 4."
        AIM-4E track tone

Time: 4+36
    Handley: "Going guns."
    Smallwood: "OK."
    Sound of M-61 Gatling gun spooling up and down while firing under
    heavy G loading
    Garbled transmissions

Time: 4+48
    Handley: "He's going down... you got him?"
    Smallwood: "Yeah."
    Handley: "I got him... I got him... He hit the ground."
        Every fighter pilot on frequency: [lots of shouting at the same time]
        Downey: "Way to go."
        Green: "Let's get out of here."

Time: 4+58
    Handley: "I got him."
        Garbled transmissions... "Let's get out of here."
        Handley: "That's the gun, baby."
        Green: "Let's get out of here, Brenda... he's... uh, closing at six
        right now."
        Straining under Gs during pull down to the east from vertical
        quarter-roll and zoom maneuver

Glossary

1V1 – One-versus-one.

3/9 line – A line drawn on an aircraft from wing to wing. A fighter pilot uses this line to determine whether an aircraft is in front or behind him.

AB – Afterburner.

ACM – Air Combat Maneuvering.

ACT – Air Combat Tactics.

AI – Airborne Intercept.

Angels – Altitude expressed in thousands of feet. For example, "Angels 20" means an altitude of 20,000 feet.

Angle-off – The difference in degrees between your aircraft's heading and a bandit's heading. Also known as Heading Crossing Angle or HCA.

Armour Star hands – Big meaty, clumsy hands. Usually apt to oversteer or improperly fly an aircraft.

Aspect angle – The number of degrees from the tail of the target to your aircraft.

Attack geometry – The path that an offensive fighter takes as he converges on a bandit.

Bar – A sweep of a radar beam.

Basic Fighter Maneuvers (BFM) – This describes how aircraft maneuver against each other in one-versus-one air combat.

Belly check – A procedure to check out what's below you by doing a 180° roll and looking where your underside was.

Boresight mode – A radar mode where the radar beam is fixed straight out the aircraft's nose. Whatever comes into its beam first is automatically locked.

Butterfly setup – A combat training entry wherein two fighters start abreast of each other and then turn 45° away from each other. After reaching a distance of four miles, the two fighters turn back to each other for a head-on pass.

BVR – Beyond visual range.

Corner velocity – The airspeed where an aircraft has the quickest turn rate with the smallest turn radius.

Crawl back up in the cockpit – At times, the pilot may experience a phenomenon called "task saturation," where too many things are going on at once. The pilot may then "fall behind" in his ability to keep up with his aircraft's actions. He'll then need to mentally crawl back up in the cockpit to regain complete control of his bird.

Dissimilar Air Combat Tactics (DACT) – An air combat engagement with multiple planes on each side, where each side's aircraft are of different characteristics (e.g., F-16s vs. F-14s).

Drag – A maneuver to 60° or less of aspect.

Energy – In BFM, it is an aircraft's maneuvering potential.

Enhanced Envelope Gun Sight (EEGS) – A new gun sight for the F-16 and F-15 aircraft. One of its most prominent features is the funnel.

Escape window – A pilot's safe path out of a fight. It represents the chance of safely separating from the fight.

Flight path marker – A three-pronged marker in the F-16's HUD that displays changes in the F-16's flight direction.

Food fight – A heated multi-plane dogfight.

Fox 2 – A radio call from a friendly aircraft announcing that he is firing an AIM-9P Sidewinder missile.

G force – Gravitational force. Each G is equivalent to one times the force of gravity.

GCI – Ground control intercept.

Gun cross – A cross on the F-16 HUD that represents the departure line for M61A1 cannon rounds.

Heading crossing angle (HCA) – The difference in degrees between your aircraft's heading and a bandit's heading. Also known as angle-off.

HEI – High explosive incendiary. The type of ammunition the F-16's M61A1 cannon fires.

High alpha – High angle of attack.

High yo-yo – A classic fighter maneuver performed out of plane.

Highway style – A head-on flyby side to side, as if passing each other on a highway.

HUD – Head-Up Display.

Hurt locker – In trouble.

ILS – Instrument Landing System. The function of the ILS is to assist the pilot in landing the F-16.

IP – Instructor pilot.

IR – Infrared.

Jink – A violent back-and-forth maneuver designed to throw off an enemy aircraft.

Kinetic energy – The velocity at which an aircraft is traveling.

Knock it off – Stop the engagement. Used as a command in training exercises to stop the current air combat fight.

L-1 maneuver – Straining maneuvers for countering G forces with the windpipe closed (glottal).

Lag pursuit – A pursuit course where you point your aircraft's nose behind a bandit. This course is primarily used when approaching a bandit.

Lead pursuit – A pursuit course where you point your aircraft's nose in front of a bandit. This course is used when you want to fire your guns at the bandit.

Lead turn – An attempt to decrease angle-off before crossing a bandit's 3/9 line. It is accomplished by judging a bandit's heading and pulling hard Gs into him without overshooting.

Level turn – A horizontal turn that reduces your airspeed at high G while turning into your opponent. It does not have as fast a turn rate as a slice, but does allow you to keep a visual on the bandit.

Lift vector – An imaginary arrow (vector) that is projected from the top of the jet perpendicular to the aircraft's wings. At high G, an aircraft moves along its lift vector.

Lufbery – A 1V1 one-circle fight where each fighter is chasing the other's tail. Usually, the first person to make a mistake or leave the fight loses. Named after the World War I American ace Raoul Lufbery.

M-1 maneuver – Straining maneuvers for countering G forces with the windpipe open (grunting).

Mach – The speed of sound (760 feet/second at sea level).

Magellan Act – To get lost and just roam around.

Magic move – A maneuver or tactic that will always work in any situation. This is a fallacy because there are never any magic moves in air combat.

Merge – The point where the opposing fighters pass each other.

Military power – 100% throttle, not entering an afterburner stage.

Missile engagement zone – An area around a bandit (modified by high G) where you can effectively fire a missile.

Mud Hen – An F-15E fitted for air-to-ground delivery of weapons.

Offensive perch setup – A BFM training setup where a fighter starts in front of another at the same elevation.

One-circle fight – A 1V1 fight where two fighters come at each other head-on and both make opposite direction turns (that is, one turns left and the other turns right). This brings both fighters turning into each other completing a circle.

Out of plane – When an aircraft does evasive maneuvers in a non-horizontal plane of movement.

Overshoot – Flying your aircraft in a manner that causes you to either fly in front of your target (a 3/9 overshoot) or way behind your target (a flight path overshoot).

Perch – A position behind the bandit from which an attack can be launched.

Positional geometry – How to determine your combat position in relation to your enemy. It consists of three elements: angle-off, range and aspect angle.

Potential energy – Stored energy that can be converted to kinetic energy. The higher the altitude, the more potential energy you have. You can always convert potential energy for speed.

Pucker factor – Anxiety level.

Pure pursuit – A pursuit course where you point your aircraft's nose directly at the bandit. This course is used to shoot missiles at the bandit.

Pure vertical – Straight up.

Radial gravity (GR) – The G force an aircraft is adding to the turn rate and radius equations. Most of the time 1 GR equates to 3°–4° per second.

Range – The distance between your aircraft and the bandit.

Rope-a-dope – Any maneuver designed to deceive the enemy.

SFO – Simulated flameout. A landing approach that simulates a flameout (engine out).

Shark killer – A missile that misses its target and plunges into the water.

Situational awareness (SA) – A pilot's ability to keep track of his surroundings and predict possible actions while in air combat.

Slave mode – Where the weapons are "slaved" to a sensor such as radar. The weapon is then focused on the same place the radar is looking.

Slice – A maximum performance, nose-low turn.

Smash – Airspeed.

Snake – A defensive maneuver designed to defeat a guns kill from behind. It consists of slowing down, in a series of turn reversals, rolling 180°, in hopes a bandit overshoots.

Snapshot – A guns shot that consists of a quick pull into lead pursuit and firing a burst of rounds across the enemy's aircraft.

Snot locker – Nose. Heading down the snot locker means the bandit is flying at you head-on.

Spike – Radar contact.

Spit out – To disengage from a battle whether voluntary or involuntary or to overshoot.

Square a corner – To make a high G maneuver that appears to be a complete right-angle turn.

TACAN – TACtical Air Navigation. A beacon designed to facilitate navigation.

Tactical intercept – A specific set of procedures taken by a fighter using radar to gain an advantage on an enemy.

Tally – A visual. As in "I have a tally on him."

Threat Warning System (TWS) – An electronic device on the F-16 that displays air and ground radars.

TOF – Time of flight.

Towel rack – A handle located on each side of the F-16 that a pilot can use to move around in the cockpit.

Tracking gun shot – A guns shot where you remain in a stable position behind a bandit and take multiple shots.

Turkey – A nickname for an F-14.

Turn circle – A path that an aircraft cuts through the sky when it turns.

Turn radius – A measure of how tight an aircraft is turning.

Turn rate – A measure of how fast an aircraft moves around a turn circle.

Turning room – The distance between your aircraft's flight path and the bandit's flight path. The more distance, the more turning room.

Two-circle fight – A 1V1 fight where two fighters come at each other head-on and make same direction turns (that is, both turn to their left) on the pass. This brings both fighters turning into each other completing two separate circles.

Uncage – Release or enable a missile seeker head to independently track the target after lock-on.

Vertical – Away from the earth. When you pull your aircraft into the vertical, you pull straight up.

VID – Visually Identify.

Weapons envelope – The area around the bandit where your missiles or gun is effective.

Winchester – Out of weapons.